Billy Graham Evangelistic Association

DEAR FRIEND,

I am pleased to send you this copy of *Day by Day with Billy Graham.*

This daily devotional compiled from my father's writings has helped many people spend daily time with God. The short readings provide godly counsel on a wide variety of topics, which are also indexed at the back.

The Billy Graham Evangelistic Association exists to take the message of Christ to all we can by every effective means available to us. Our desire is to introduce as many as we can to the person of Jesus Christ, so that they might experience His love and forgiveness.

Your prayers are the most important way to support us in this ministry. We are grateful for the dedicated prayer support we receive. We are also grateful for those who support us with contributions.

If you would like to know more about the Billy Graham Evangelistic Association, please contact us:

In the U.S.:

Billy Graham Evangelistic Association
1 Billy Graham Parkway
Charlotte, North Carolina 28201-0001
www.billygraham.org
Toll-free: 1-877-2GRAHAM
(1-877-247-2426)

In Canada:

Billy Graham Evangelistic Association of Canada
20 Hopewell Way NE
Calgary, Alberta T3J 5H5
www.billygraham.ca
Toll-free: 1-888-393-0003

We would appreciate knowing how this book or our ministry has touched your life. May God bless you.

Sincerely,

Franklin Graham
President

STEPS TO PEACE WITH GOD

1. **RECOGNIZE GOD'S PLAN—PEACE AND LIFE**

   The message in this book stresses that God loves you and wants you to experience His peace and life.

   The BIBLE says . . . For God loved the world so much that He gave His only Son, so that everyone who believes in Him may not die but have eternal life. John 3:16

2. **REALIZE OUR PROBLEM—SEPARATION**

   People choose to disobey God and go their own way. This results in separation from God.

   The BIBLE says . . . Everyone has sinned and is far away from God's saving presence. Romans 3:23

3. **RESPOND TO GOD'S REMEDY—CROSS OF CHRIST**

   God sent His Son to bridge the gap. Christ did this by paying the penalty of our sins when He died on the cross and rose from the grave.

   The BIBLE says . . . But God has shown us how much He loves us—it was while we were still sinners that Christ died for us! Romans 5:8

4. **RECEIVE GOD'S SON—LORD AND SAVIOR**

   You cross the bridge into God's family when you ask Christ to come into your life.

   The BIBLE says . . . Some, however, did receive Him and believed in Him; so He gave them the right to become God's children. John 1:12

THE INVITATION IS TO:

REPENT (turn from your sins) and by faith RECEIVE Jesus Christ into your heart and life and follow Him in obedience as your Lord and Savior.

PRAYER OF COMMITMENT

"Lord Jesus, I know I am a sinner. I believe You died for my sins. Right now, I turn from my sins and open the door of my heart and life. I receive You as my personal Lord and Savior. Thank You for saving me now. Amen."

If you are committing your life to Christ, please let us know!
Billy Graham Evangelistic Association
1 Billy Graham Parkway, Charlotte, NC 28201-0001
1-877-2GRAHAM (1-877-247-2426)
www.billygraham.org

DAY BY DAY
with
Billy Graham

This **Billy Graham Library Selection** special edition
is published by the Billy Graham Evangelistic Association.

Compiled and edited by
Joan Winmill Brown

A **Billy Graham Library Selection** designates materials that are appropriate to a well-rounded collection of quality Christian literature, including both classic and contemporary reading and reference materials.

Acknowledgements

Quotations from: *World Aflame*, Copyright © 1965, by Billy Graham. Crusade edition published by arrangement with Doubleday & Company, Inc., 501 Franklin Ave., Garden City, N.Y. 11531; *Peace With God*, Copyright © 1953, by Billy Graham. Published by Doubleday & Company, Inc., 501 Franklin Ave., Garden City, N.Y. 11531; *The Secret of Happiness*, Copyright © 1955 by Billy Graham. Published by Doubleday & Company, Inc., 501 Franklin Ave., Garden City, N.Y. 11531; *The Jesus Generation*, © 1971 by Billy Graham. Published by Zondervan Publishing House, 1415 Lake Drive, S.E., Grand Rapids, Michigan 49506; *My Answer*, Copyright © 1960 by Billy Graham. Published by Doubleday & Company, Inc., 501 Franklin Ave., Garden City, N.Y. 11531; *The Challenge*, Copyright © 1969 by Billy Graham. Published by Doubleday & Company, Inc., 501 Franklin Ave., Garden City, N.Y. 11531; *Billy Graham Answers Your Questions*. Published 1968 by World Wide Publications, P.O. Box 668089, Charlotte, North Carolina 28266; *The Wit and Wisdom of Billy Graham*, Copyright © 1967 by Bill Adler. Published by Random House, Inc., 457 Madison, New York, N.Y. 10022. Sermon Excerpts from DECISION magazine & booklets copyrighted by the Billy Graham Evangelistic Association, 1 Billy Graham Parkway, Charlotte, North Carolina 28201.

Scripture from King James Version and *The Living Bible*, © 1971 by Tyndale House Publishers, Wheaton, Illinois. Used by permission.

Day by Day with Billy Graham, compiled and edited by Joan Winmill Brown, Copyright © 1976 by the Billy Graham Evangelistic Association.

Printed in the United States of America.

ISBN 0-913367-45-1
Previously ISBN 0-89066-056-5

FOREWORD

Whenever Billy Graham preaches a sermon or writes a book, he presents a clear uncompromising message of the Gospel, which results in great numbers of people coming to know Jesus Christ as their Lord and Savior. In addition to the emphasis on redemption, however, his words also cover other subjects that affect each one of us as we live from day to day—such subjects as love for our fellowman, loneliness, joy, depression, guilt, and victorious Christian living, to name a few.

I have heard Billy Graham preach on innumerable occasions over the years as I accompanied my husband to many parts of the world in his former work as Crusade Director for Dr. Graham. Always I have been deeply impressed with the many varied thoughts contained in every sermon. From these and from Dr. Graham's major writings, I have compiled the devotional thoughts contained in this book.

To each devotional I have added a related Scripture verse, and I have written a prayer to encourage those who, like me, desire a closer walk with our Lord and want to know His guidance.

I am deeply grateful to Dr. Graham for his permission to use this material. My thanks to Ginny Booth who has so faithfully assisted in the typing and research.

Joan Winmill Brown

•JANUARY 1•

". . . Forgetting the past and
looking forward to what lies ahead."
Philippians 3:13 (TLB)

As we flick the calendar to a New Year, we come face to face with the fact that our days on earth are numbered. As the Psalmist wrote, "Teach us to number our days, that we may apply our hearts unto wisdom." No thoughtful person can approach New Year's Day without some introspection. We are reminded of the brevity of time. We also look back over our failures, mistakes, and missed opportunities, and vow that we will make better use of our time during the coming year. We should take time to be pleasant, to smile, to extend the small courtesies we often omit—to show love to our family. Psychiatrists tell us that most people are starved for love. Take time for the goodbye kiss; we shall go to work with a sweeter spirit. Let us take time to get acquainted with our families. We are not machines. We are not robots. The secret of a happy home is that members of the family learn to give and receive love. Let us take time to express our love in a thousand ways.

Prayer For The Day:

As I begin a New Year, Lord Jesus,
I pray that my walk through the days ahead will
be filled with Your love for others, a love that does not
count the cost.

•JANUARY 2•

"O God, thou art my God; early will
I seek thee; my soul thirsteth for thee . . ."
Psalm 63:1

Some Christians have learned little of a daily devotional life. Some time ago a policeman asked me what the secret of victorious living was. I told him that there is no magic formula that can be pronounced. If any word could describe it, I would say *surrender*. The second word I would say would be *devotion*. Nothing can take the place of a daily devotional life with Christ. Your quiet time, your prayer time, the time you spend in the Word, is absolutely essential for a happy Christian life. You cannot possibly be a happy, dynamic, and powerful Christian apart from a daily walk with Christ. Christ is calling Christians today to cleansing, to dedication, to consecration, and to full surrender. It will make the difference between success and failure in your spiritual life. It will make the difference between being helped and helping others. It will make a difference in your habits, in your prayer life, in your Bible reading, in your giving, in your testimony, and in your church membership. This is the Christian hour of decision!

Prayer For The Day:

> *I long for a deeper devotional life,*
> *living Lord. May I consecrate myself completely to You.*

•JANUARY 3•

> *"As the Father hath loved me,*
> *so have I loved you: continue ye in my love."*
> John 15:9

The great Swiss theologian, Dr. Karl Barth, was probably in his generation the greatest theologian in the world, and a great philosopher as well. I did not always agree with him, but he was my friend and I respected him. While he was in this country, a student at one of the seminaries said, "Dr. Barth, what is the greatest truth that ever crossed your mind?" All the seminary students were sitting on the edge of their seats to hear some great, profound, deep, complicated answer. Dr. Barth slowly raised his great shaggy gray head and looked at the student and said, "Jesus loves me, this I know, for the Bible tells me so."

Prayer For The Day:

> *Lord Jesus, may I always keep*
> *the knowledge of Your love in true simplicity—*
> *unencumbered by much learning. Thank You for loving me.*

•JANUARY 4•

> *"The Lord is my light*
> *and my salvation; whom shall I fear?"*
> Psalm 27:1

Today many people are living in the bondage of fear. In a recent study a psychiatrist said that the greatest problem facing his patients was fear. Fear of going insane, committing suicide, being alone, or fear of heart disease, cancer, disaster, or death. We are becoming a nation of fearful people. Down through the centuries in times of trouble, temptation, trial, bereavement, and crisis, God has brought courage to the hearts of those who love Him. The Bible is crowded with assurances of God's help and comfort in every kind of trouble which might cause fears to arise in the human heart. Today the Christian can come to the Scriptures with full assurance that God is going to deliver the person who puts his trust and confidence in God. Christians can look into the future with promise, hope, and joy, and without fear, discouragement, or despondency.

Prayer For The Day:

Your assurances of love still the fears of my heart, Lord.

·JANUARY 5·

"Love never faileth . . ."

1 Corinthians 13:8

The first essential for a happy Christian home is that love must be practiced. Homes that are built on animal attraction and lust are destined to crumble and fall. Love is the cohesive force that holds the family together. True love contains an element of spiritual mystery. It embodies loyalty, reverence, and understanding. Love imposes a tremendous responsibility on all members of a family, but it is a responsibility accompanied by glorious rewards. "Love," says the Bible, "even as Christ . . . loved the church, and gave Himself for it." How did Christ love the church? He loved it despite its faults, its mistakes, and its weaknesses. True love does not fail. It loves despite personality defects, physical blemishes, and mental quirks. Love is deep, abiding, and eternal. Nothing can bring a sense of security into the home as true love can.

Prayer For The Day:

Help me today, to listen, to love and care
for my loved ones with a heart that is made sensitive by You, Jesus.

·JANUARY 6·

"Keep a sharp lookout! For you do not know
when I will come. . . . Watch for my return!"
Mark 13:35,36 (TLB)

The great Dwight L. Moody used to say, "I never preach a sermon without thinking that possibly the Lord may come before I preach another." Dr. G. Campbell Morgan, the distinguished British clergyman, said, "I never begin my work in the morning without thinking that perhaps He may interrupt my work and begin His own. I am not looking for death. I am looking for Him." That is the way a Christian should live his life—in the constant anticipation of the return of Jesus Christ! If we could live every day as though it might be the very last one before the final judgment, what a difference it would make here on earth! But we don't like to think that way. We don't like to think that our carefully made plans, our long-range schemes may be interrupted by the trumpet of God. Too many people would rather say, "Oh, well, the end of the world hasn't come yet, so why think about it—it's probably a thousand years away."

Prayer For The Day:

Today might be the day
when Jesus returns. Cleanse me, Father.

·JANUARY 7·

"He is my refuge . . ."

Psalm 91:2

Modern psychiatrists say that one of the basic needs of man is security. In the 91st Psalm we are assured that in God we have the greatest of security, "There shall no evil befall thee, neither shall any plague come nigh thy dwelling. For He shall give His angels charge over thee, to keep thee in all thy ways." If you read and reread this beautiful Psalm, you will discover that in Him we have a permanent abode and residence, and that all of the comfort, security, and affection which the human heart craves is found in Him. Perhaps no visible angels will appear in your life and mine, but God's promise of security is nonetheless real and certain. Those who live in the realm of God have genuine safety and security.

Prayer For The Day:

Wherever I go this day,
You and Your angels will be with me.
Thank You, Lord, for the peace, love, and security You promise.

•JANUARY 8•

"What things soever ye
desire, when ye pray, believe . . ."

Mark 11:24

W e are to pray in times of adversity, lest we become faithless and unbelieving. We are to pray in times of prosperity, lest we become boastful and proud. We are to pray in times of danger, lest we become fearful and doubting. We need to pray in times of security, lest we become self-sufficient. Sinners, pray to a merciful God for forgiveness. Christians, pray for an outpouring of God's Spirit upon a willful, evil, unrepentant world. Parents, pray that God may crown your home with grace and mercy. Children, pray for the salvation of your parents. Christians, saints of God, pray that the dew of heaven may fall on earth's dry thirsty ground, and that righteousness may cover the earth as the waters cover the sea.

Prayer For The Day:

Let me pour everything out to You, Lord.
Thank You for the knowledge that You hear me!

•JANUARY 9•

"Despise God's Word and find
yourself in trouble. Obey it and succeed."

Proverbs 13:13 (TLB)

A s Christians, we have the Spirit of God in us. But ours is the responsibility to keep sin out of our lives so that the Spirit can produce His fruit in us. Become grounded in the Bible. As Christians, we have only one authority, one compass: the Word of God. Abraham Lincoln in a letter to a friend said, "I am profitably engaged in reading the Bible. Take all of this Book upon reason that you can, and the balance upon faith. You will live and die a better man." Begin the day with the Book; and as the day comes to a close, let the Word speak its wisdom to your soul. Let it be the firm foundation upon which your hope is built. Let it be the Staff of Life upon which your spirit is nourished. Let it be the Sword of the Spirit which cuts away the evil of your life and fashions you in His image and likeness.

Prayer For The Day:

Almighty God, Your Word
nourishes my whole being and I praise Your holy name!

•JANUARY 10•

"From everlasting
to everlasting, thou art God."

Psalm 90:2

Have you ever thought about the collapse of time? From the days of the Lord Jesus Christ until about 1830, man could not travel any faster than a horse. In 1960, a man went into space and traveled at a speed of 18,000 miles an hour. Look how far we have come in so short a time! Sometimes when I read the papers, I think we are trying to run the Space Age with horse-and-buggy moral and spiritual equipment. Technology, you see, has no morals; and with no moral restraints man will destroy himself ecologically, militarily, or in some other way. Only God can give a person moral restraints and spiritual strength. While our world is shaking and crumbling, we need to realize that one thing will never change, and that is God. He is the same today as He was ten million years ago, and He will be the same ten million years from today. We are like grasshoppers; we appear and hop around a bit on the earth, and then we are gone.

Prayer For The Day:

Almighty God, to know You
are unchanging gives me peace in a frighteningly changing world.

·JANUARY 11·

*"What we suffer now is nothing
compared to the glory he will give us later."*

Romans 8:18 (TLB)

Nowhere does the Bible teach that Christians are to be exempt from the tribulations and natural disasters that come upon the world. It does teach that the Christian can face tribulation, crisis, calamity, and personal suffering with a supernatural power that is not available to the person outside Christ. The early Christians were able to experience joy in their hearts in the midst of trials, troubles, and depression. They counted suffering for Christ not as a burden or misfortune, but as a great honor, as evidence that Christ counted them worthy to witness to Him through suffering. They never forgot what Christ Himself had gone through for their salvation; and to suffer for His name's sake was regarded as a gift rather than a cross. Christians can rejoice in tribulation because they have eternity's values in view. When the pressures are on, they look beyond their present predicaments to the glories of heaven. The thought of the future life with its prerogatives and joys helps to make the trials of the present seem light and transient.

Prayer For The Day:

*Father, help me to go beyond
the afflictions and tribulations of our age,
and to look toward the inheritance reserved for us in heaven.*

·JANUARY 12·

*"Most gladly therefore will I rather
glory in my infirmities, that the power of Christ
may rest upon me."*

2 Corinthians 12:9

God is especially close to us when we are lying on a sickbed. God will make the bed soft and will freshen it with His presence and with His tender care. He makes the bed comfortable and wipes away our tears. He ministers to us with special tenderness at such a time and reveals His great love for us. Tell me why the gardener trims and prunes his rosebushes, sometimes cutting away productive branches, and I will tell you why God's people are afflicted. God's hand never slips. He never makes a mistake. His every move is for our own good and for our ultimate good. Oftentimes He must deform us and mutilate our own image. Deformity sometimes precedes conformity.

Prayer For The Day:

> *When times of tribulation come,*
> *help me, dear Lord, to glory in them for Your sake.*

•JANUARY 13•

> *"And now, Lord,*
> *what wait I for? my hope is in thee."*
> *Psalm 39:7*

The sea was beating against the rocks in huge, dashing waves. The lightning was flashing, the thunder was roaring, the wind was blowing; but the little bird was asleep in the crevice of the rock, its head serenely under its wing, sound asleep. That is peace—to be able to sleep in the storm! In Christ, we are relaxed and at peace in the midst of the confusion, bewilderments, and perplexities of life. The storm rages, but our hearts are at rest. We have found peace—at last!

Prayer For The Day:

> *Thank You, dear Lord, for the hope*
> *I have in Your abiding love, which surrounds me.*

•JANUARY 14•

> *"I am the good shepherd, and*
> *know my sheep, and am known of mine."*
> *John 10:14*

Unless God is revealed to us through personal experience, we can never really know God. Most of us know *about* God, but that is quite different from knowing God. We learn about God through the agencies of the church, the Sunday school, the youth activities, the worship services. Many people stop in their quest for God at this point. It is one thing to be introduced to a person, but quite another thing to know him personally.

Prayer For The Day:

*Lord, You are, indeed, the
good Shepherd, who leads me each day. Help me to love
and know You more deeply so that others may be drawn
into Your fold.*

•JANUARY 15•

*"When my heart is overwhelmed:
lead me to the rock that is higher than I."*

Psalm 61:2

When you become a Christian, it doesn't mean that you will live on a perpetual "high." The Psalmist David went down to the very depths, and so did the Apostle Paul. But in the midst of all circumstances God's grace, peace, and joy are there. The tears will still come, the pressures will be felt, and so will the temptations. But there is a new dimension, a new direction, and a new power in life to face the circumstances in which you live.

Prayer For The Day:

*David and Paul have given me the example of trusting You,
Lord, even in the excruciating valleys of life.
Like them, I praise You.*

•JANUARY 16•

*"I will rejoice in the Lord,
I will joy in the God of my salvation."*

Habakkuk 3:18

Christians are supposed to be happy persons! Our generation has become well versed in Christian terminology, but is remiss in the actual practice of Christ's principles and teachings. Hence, our greatest need today is not more Christianity but more true Christians. The world can argue against Christianity as an institution, but there is no convincing argument against a person who, through the Spirit of God, has been made Christlike. Such a person is a living rebuke to the selfishness, rationalism, and materialism of the day. Jesus said to the woman at Jacob's well, "Whosoever drinketh of the water that I shall give him shall never thirst."

This sin-sick, disillusioned woman was the symbol of the whole race. Her longings were our longings! Her heart-cry was our heart-cry! Her disillusionment was our disillusionment! Her sin was our sin! But her Savior can be our Savior! Her forgiveness can be our forgiveness! Her joy can be our joy!

Prayer For The Day:

> *My soul delights in You, my God, and my Redeemer.*

·JANUARY 17·

> *"And ye shall know the truth,*
> *and the truth shall make you free."*
> *John 8:32*

Ours is an age of philosophical uncertainty, and we no longer know what we believe. We stand uncommitted. Everywhere I go, I ask students, "What is controlling you?" When I was a student, I had to face Christ. Who was He? He had made the astounding claim, "I am the way, the truth, and the life. No man cometh unto the Father but by me." I wrestled with the inescapable fact that either Jesus Christ was who He claimed to be, or He was the biggest liar, fraud and charlatan in history. Which was it? Buddha said toward the end of his life, "I am still searching for truth." But here was Jesus who appeared and said, "I am the embodiment of all truth. All truth is centered in me."

Prayer For The Day:

> *Thank You, Jesus,*
> *for my freedom—because You are the Truth!*

·JANUARY 18·

> *"To open their eyes and to*
> *turn them from darkness to light . . ."*
> *Acts 26:18*

The blind man, Bartimaeus, threw off his cloak and ran trembling to Jesus. And Jesus said, "What do you want me to do for you?" He said, "Lord, that I may receive my sight." In that moment as he said, "Lord," his spiritual eyes were opened. And Jesus said, "Your faith has made you whole." Notice—not your intellectual understanding, not your money, not your works—but your faith. Faith! That's all it takes! Immediately Bartimaeus, who had been blind all of his life, began to open his eyes, and the first thing he saw was the face of Jesus. What an experience—to open one's eyes and look straight into the strong, tender face of Jesus! Bartimaeus met Jesus and the record says he "followed Jesus in the way." When you go back to your business, or your home, or your neighborhood, or your friends, or your school, you don't go alone. Christ goes with you.

Prayer For The Day:

Thank You, Lord Jesus,
for healing me from my spiritual blindness!

•JANUARY 19•

"Happy is he . . .
whose hope is in the Lord his God."

Psalm 146:5

Happy is the man who has learned the secret of coming to God in daily prayer. Fifteen minutes alone with God every morning before you start the day can change circumstances and remove mountains! But all of this happiness and all of these unlimited benefits which flow from the storehouse of heaven are contingent upon our relationship to God. Absolute dependency and absolute yieldedness are the conditions of being His child. Only His children are entitled to receive those things that lend themselves to happiness; and in order to be His child, there must be the surrender of the will to Him. Man does not come to know God through works—he comes to know God by faith, through grace. You cannot work your way toward happiness and heaven, you cannot moralize your way, you cannot reform your way, you cannot buy your way. It comes as a gift of God through Christ.

Prayer For The Day:

Thank You, heavenly Father, for the gift
of joy which comes from knowing Your Son, Jesus Christ.

·JANUARY 20·

"For he knoweth our frame . . ."
Psalm 103:14

I t is significant that our first astronauts, while being trained for their moon flights, were required to give twenty answers to the query, "Who are you?" Take the same test yourself. When you have made your list and run out of things to add, ask yourself if you have truly answered? Do you really know who you are? Scientists agree that our desperate search leads all humans to seek heroes and to imitate others, to "paste bits and pieces of other people on ourselves." We make love as some actor would. We play golf in the style of Jack Nicklaus. Part of this process is natural, for we learn by imitating others. The tragedy is that the person we assemble is not genuine. "Who am I?" you cry as you roam the world looking for yourself. Consider this: there are three of you. There is the person you think you are. There is the person others think you are. There is the person God knows you are and can be through Christ.

Prayer For The Day:

*Lord, help me to break through
the facade and know myself as You do.*

·JANUARY 21·

"O death, where is thy sting? . . ."
1 Corinthians 15:55

D eath is the most democratic experience in life for we all participate in it. We think of its happening only to other people. We don't like to grow old and we don't like to die. The Bible teaches that death is an enemy of man and God. But it also teaches that this enemy, death, will ultimately be destroyed forever; that in fact it has already been defeated at the cross and resurrection of Jesus Christ. Death, for a Christian, brings permanent freedom from evil. It also means the believer will be like Jesus. We shall be like Christ in love. So much of self is involved in what we do here; but one day, in Christ, we will have perfect love. What a glorious time it will be when we get to heaven!

Prayer For The Day:

*Jesus, Your victory over death
comforts my heart and fills me with hope.*

·JANUARY 22·

"But the angel of the Lord by night opened
the prison doors, and brought them forth . . ."
Acts 5:19

Demonic activity and Satan worship are on the increase in all parts of the world. The devil is at work more than at any other time. The Bible says that because he realizes his time is short, Satan's activity will increase. But his evil activities are countered for the people of God by His ministering spirits, the holy ones of the angelic order. Christians should never fail to sense the operation of angelic glory. It forever eclipses the world of demonic powers, as the sun does a candle's light. If you are a believer, expect powerful angels to accompany you in your life experiences. And let those events dramatically illustrate the friendly presence of "the holy ones" as Daniel calls them. Certainly, the eye of faith sees many evidences of the supernatural display of God's power and glory. God is still in business.

Prayer For The Day:

When I am tempted by Satan,
I will remember Your angels are around me, Lord.

·JANUARY 23·

"Glory in the Lord; O worshipers of God,
rejoice. Search for him and for his strength,
and keep on searching!"
Psalm 105:3,4 (TLB)

Jerome, one of the early Christians, said, "Ignorance of the Bible means ignorance of Christ." Job once said, "I have esteemed the words of his mouth more than my necessary food." Jeremiah said, "Thy words were found and I did eat them; and thy word was unto me the joy and rejoicing of mine heart." To read the Bible one needs a "quiet time." Christian students often ask, "How do you maintain your spiritual high? What do you do on a daily basis?" I tell them about my "quiet time." Some days it is in the early—sometimes late—morning, sometimes evening. Without it, my Christian life would be a wilderness. Isaiah said, "They that wait upon the Lord shall renew their strength; they shall mount up with wings as eagles, they shall run, and not be weary; and they shall walk, and not faint" (Isaiah 40:31). So gain the strength of eagles, as the prophet suggested. Set a time each day when you can spend a few minutes alone with God.

Prayer For The Day:

*Dear Lord, teach us
to wait upon You, that we may know Your strength.*

•JANUARY 24•

"Go and make disciples in all the nations . . ."
Matthew 28:19 (TLB)

C hristian missions is unique in the aggressive movements of history. Christianity in its pure form has no "axe to grind," no system to foster, and no profit motivation. Its job is simply to "seek and to save that which is lost." Nothing more, nothing less. The words "apostle" and "missionary" mean the same thing: "One who is sent." The word apostle is from the Greek; and the word missionary is from the Latin. The New Testament is a book of missions. The Gospels tell of Jesus' missionary accomplishments, and the Acts tell of the missionary endeavors of the apostles. The disciples were launched into the world by the power of the resurrection, and the Gospel made its impact upon the world's people. Peter went to Lydda, Joppa, Antioch, Babylon, and Asia Minor. John went to Samaria, Ephesus, and to the cities on the Mediterranean. Thomas journeyed to far away India. Paul, the peer of all early missionaries, used the roads Rome had built to take the Gospel through the Empire. Today the need for missions is greater than ever before! The world is shrinking in size but expanding in population. We live in a world of conflicting, confusing beliefs! We live in a world of complex problems! But, more important, we live in a world of dire spiritual need.

Prayer For The Day:

*Father, help me to be a light
in this world of darkness, ready for each opportunity
to share Your love with those whose spiritual needs are great.*

·JANUARY 25·

*"But God commendeth his love
toward us, in that, while we were yet
sinners, Christ died for us."*

Romans 5:8

As we stand at the cross of Christ we see a glorious exhibition of God's love. Paul wrote to the Christians in Rome, "While we were powerless to help ourselves . . . Christ died for sinful men." In human experience, it is a rare thing for one man to give his life for another, even if the latter be a good man, though there have been a few who have had the courage to do it. Yet the proof of God's amazing love is this: that it was "while we were sinners Christ died for us." A beautiful young society leader came to visit my wife and me. She had been converted to Christ in one of our Crusades, and she was absolutely radiant in her transformation. Already she had learned scores of Scripture verses by heart and was so full of Christ that we sat for two hours listening to her give her moving testimony. Over and over she said, "I cannot understand how God could forgive me. I have been such a wicked sinner. I just cannot understand the love of God."

Prayer For The Day:

*It is beyond comprehension
the love that took You to the cross for me.
Humbly I praise and thank You, my Savior and my Lord.*

·JANUARY 26·

*"We work hard and suffer much in order
that people will believe it, for our hope is in the
living God who died for all . . ."*

1 Timothy 4:9,10 (TLB)

Our life has its beginning in suffering. Life's span is marked by pain and tragedy, and our lives terminate with the enemy called death. The person who expects to escape the pangs of suffering and disappointment simply has no knowledge of the Bible, of history, or of life. The master musician knows that suffering precedes glory and acclaim. He knows the hours, days, and months of grueling practice and self-sacrifice that precede the one hour of perfect rendition when his mastership is applauded. The student knows that years of study, privation and self-renunciation precede the triumphant day of graduation and honors. Yes, there are clouds of suffering for each one of us, but God says, "I come to you in the thick dark cloud of suffering." By faith you can see His blessed face in the storm. God has His plan and purpose in all suffering.

Prayer For The Day:

Heavenly Father, help me to remember that none of my suffering is in vain. Through it teach me more of Your love and comfort.

•JANUARY 27•

"Bless me and my family forever!"
2 Samuel 7:29 (TLB)

A part from religious influence, the family is the most important unit of society. It would be good if every home were Christian, but we know that it is not so. The family and the home can never exert their proper influence while ignoring the biblical standard. The Bible calls for discipline and a recognition of authority. If children do not learn this at home, they will go out into society without the proper attitude toward authority and law. There is always the exceptional child, but the average tells us that the child is largely what the home has made him. The only way to provide the right home for your children is to put the Lord above them, and fully instruct them in the ways of the Lord. You are responsible before God for the home you provide for them.

Prayer For The Day:

Father, keep me from any word
or deed that might hinder a child from loving You.

•JANUARY 28•

". . . our Lord Jesus Christ . . . which
hath loved us . . . comfort your hearts . . ."
2 Thessalonians 2:16,17

C hrist is the answer to sorrow. When Harry Lauder, the great Scottish comedian, received word that his son had been killed in France, he said, "In a time like this, there are three courses open to man: He may give way to despair and become bitter. He may endeavor to drown his sorrow in drink or in a life of wickedness. Or he may turn to God." In your sorrow, turn to God. There are thousands of people who have turned to God, but you may be still carrying your burdens. God begs of you, "Cast all your care on me, for I care for you" (1 Peter 5:7). You who must go through the valley of the shadow of death, you who must say goodbye to those whom you have loved, you who suffer privation and misery, you who are unjustly persecuted for righteousness' sake—take heart, take courage. Our Christ is more than adequate for sorrow.

Prayer For The Day:

In sorrow, Jesus, Your comfort
will take all the bitterness and longing
away and give me courage to face the heartache. Your grace
will console me and Your arms will support me.
Thank You, dear Lord.

•JANUARY 29•

"I will declare thy name unto my brethren . . ."
Psalm 22:22

There are those near you in your own community who need the regenerating power of Christ. You can call them by name. I suggest that you make a list and begin by spending time in prayer for them. Ask God to show you how to witness to them and how to win them. Their lives can be transformed by the message you give them. You are to share this Gospel you have received. If Christ has done anything for you, then share it. In so doing, you are showing mercy! As you have received the mercy of God by the forgiveness of sin and the promise of eternal life—thus you are to show mercy! And in showing mercy you will not only receive mercy but you will find a stimulating happiness!

Prayer For The Day:

As I close my eyes in prayer, let me see
the faces of those who need to know You, beloved Savior.

·JANUARY 30·

"For what is your life? It is even
a vapour, that appeareth for a little time,
and then vanisheth away."

James 4:14

Nothing takes God by surprise. Everything is moving according to a plan; and God wants you in that plan. The devil also has a plan for the world. God has a plan and the devil has a plan, and you will have to decide which plan you are going to fit into. Scripture says that God allows us 70 years and some beyond. The first 15 years are spent in childhood and early adolescence. Twenty years are spent in bed; and in the last five, physical limitations start to curtail our activities. That gives us about 30 years in which to live as adults. We take time out for eating, and for figuring our taxes, and we are down to perhaps 15 years. Now suppose we spend seven of those years watching television. That cuts us down to seven or eight years. Our time is short! The time we can invest for God, in creative things, in reaching our fellowmen for Christ, is short!

Prayer For The Day:

Each hour of every day that is left
of this earthly life, I would spend serving You,
Lord Jesus. Forgive the time spent so often in needless endeavor.

·JANUARY 31·

"For to me to live
is Christ, and to die is gain."

Philippians 1:21

Helen Keller, who is a classic example of handling life's handicaps, said, "I thank God for my handicaps, for through them I have found myself, my work, and my God." Some people with handicaps drown themselves in self-pity, and thus limit their usefulness and service to mankind and to God. The Apostle Paul knew the pangs of suffering. He *used* his infirmity rather than allowing his infirmity to use him, and he used it for the glory of God. He seized everything, even death, to glorify his Lord. No matter which way fate turned, he was one jump ahead of it, and using it to magnify his Savior.

⋆FEBRUARY 1⋆

"We know that
all things work together for good
to them that love God . . ."

Romans 8:28

We might never have had the songs of Fanny Crosby had she not been afflicted with blindness. George Matheson would never have given the world his immortal song, "O Love That Will Not Let Me Go," had it not been for his passing through the furnace of affliction. The "Hallelujah Chorus" was written by George Frederick Handel when he was poverty-stricken and suffering from a paralyzed right side and right arm. Affliction may be for our edification and Christian development. Sickness is one of the "all things" which work together for good to them that love God. Don't resent it. Don't be embittered by it.

Prayer For The Day:

You do not make mistakes, Father.
If sorrow comes into my life,
let me use it to help others know about You.

⋆FEBRUARY 2⋆

"In hope of eternal life,
which God, that cannot lie,
promised before the world began."

Titus 1:2

Life is a glorious opportunity, if it is used to condition us for eternity. It we fail in this, though we succeed in everything else, our life will have been a failure. There is no escape for the man who squanders his opportunity to prepare to meet God. Our lives are also immortal. God made man different from the other creatures. He made him in His own image, a living soul. When this body dies and our earthly existence is terminated, the soul lives on forever. One thousand years from this day, you will be more alive than you are at this moment. The Bible teaches that life does not end at the cemetery. There is a future life with God for those who put their trust in His Son, Jesus Christ.

Prayer For The Day:

> *Thank You for eternal life in Christ and for*
> *the peace that comes over*
> *me because of this triumphant promise!*
> *Today help me relay this joyous news to those around me.*

◆FEBRUARY 3◆

> *"Create in me a new, clean heart, O God, filled*
> *with clean thoughts and right desires."*
> *Psalm 51:10 (TLB)*

You were created in the image and likeness of God. You were made for God's fellowship, and your heart can never be satisfied without His communion. Just as iron is attracted to a magnet, the soul in its state of hunger is drawn to God. Though you, like thousands of others, may feel in the state of sin that the world is more alluring and more to your liking, some day—perhaps even now as you read these words—you will acknowledge that there is something deep down inside you which cannot be satisfied by the alloy of earth. Then with David, the Psalmist who had sampled the delicacies of sin and had found them unsatisfying, you will say, "Oh, God, thou art my God; early will I seek thee: my soul thirsteth for thee, my flesh longeth for thee in a dry and thirsty land, where no water is."

Prayer For The Day:

> *How I long for You, God, yet so often my heart*
> *is drawn away from Your leading. Like David,*
> *I desire a clean heart.*

·FEBRUARY 4·

*"If I ascend up
into heaven, thou art there . . ."*

Psalm 139:8

I believe it is possible to know what God is like. The Bible declares that God is Spirit, that He is not limited to body; He is not limited to shape; He is not limited to force; He is not limited to boundaries or bonds; He is absolutely immeasurable. Thousands of people are trying to limit God to certain spheres, and relegate Him to certain categories that are the product of their own speculation. There is no limit to God. There is no limit to His wisdom. There is no limit to His power. There is no limit to His love. There is no limit to His mercy. Men change, fashions change, conditions and circumstances change, but God never changes.

Prayer For The Day:

*I limit You so many times, Lord.
Forgive my finite mind and fill me with Your wisdom,
power and mercy, so that I can touch those You love this day.*

·FEBRUARY 5·

*"Not forsaking the
assembling of ourselves together . . ."*

Hebrews 10:25

I will not argue with you about nature inspiring thoughts of God. David said, "The heavens declare the glory of God, and the firmament showeth His handiwork." But at the same time, I would give you no comfort about absenting yourself from the house of God. The Bible says, "Christ loved the Church and gave Himself for it." If our Lord loved it enough to die for it, then we should respect it enough to support and attend it. I like what Theodore Roosevelt once said, "You may worship God anywhere, at any time, but the chances are that you will not do so unless you have first learned to worship Him somewhere in some particular place, at some particular time."

Prayer For The Day:

*Down through the years,
beloved Lord, Christians have met to worship You.
Thank You that I am part of this blessed family.*

·FEBRUARY 6·

*"For if the blood of bulls and of goats . . .
sanctifieth to the purifying of the flesh; how
much more shall the blood of Christ, . . . purge
your conscience from dead works
to serve the living God?"*

Hebrews 9:13,14

To have a guilty conscience is an experience. Psychologists may define it as a guilt complex and may seek to rationalize away the sense of guilt; but once this has been awakened through the application of the law of God, no explanation will quiet the insistent voice of conscience. Many a criminal has finally given himself over to the authorities because the accusations of a guilty conscience were worse than prison bars. The Bible teaches that Christ cleanses the conscience. To have a guilty conscience cleansed and to be free from its constant accusation is an experience, but it is not the cleansing of the conscience that saves you; it is faith in Christ that saves, and a cleansed conscience is the result of having come into the right relationship with God.

Prayer For The Day:

I stand in awe of the magnitude of Your forgiveness, Father.

·FEBRUARY 7·

*"But if someone who is supposed to be
a Christian has money enough to live well,
and sees a brother in need, and won't help
him—how can God's love be within him?"*

1 John 3:17 (TLB)

You know that the hardest thing for you to give up is your money. It represents your time, your energy, your talents, your total personality converted into currency. We usually hold on to it tenaciously, yet it is uncertain in value and we cannot take it into the next world. The Scripture teaches that we are stewards for a little while of all we earn. If we misuse it, as did the man who buried his talent, it brings upon us the severest judgment of God. The tithe is the Lord's. If you use it for yourself, you are robbing God. We are to take the tithe as a standard, but to go beyond the tithe is an indication of our gratefulness for God's gifts to us. In the midst of sorrow and trouble, this life has many blessings and enjoyments which have come from the hand of God. Even our capacity for love is a gift from God. We show our gratitude by giving back to Him a part of that which He has given to us.

Prayer For The Day:

> *Give me a generous heart, Father, that does not*
> *grudgingly give back to You all that is rightfully Yours.*

·FEBRUARY 8·

> *"Those who belong to Christ have*
> *nailed their natural evil desires to his cross and*
> *crucified them there."*
>
> *Galatians 5:24 (TLB)*

The strength for our conquering and our victory is drawn continually from Christ. The Bible does not teach that sin is completely eradicated from the Christian in this life, but it does teach that sin shall no longer reign over you. The strength and power of sin have been broken. The Christian now has resources available to live above and beyond this world. The Bible teaches that whosoever is born of God does not practice sin. It is like the little girl who said that when the devil came knocking with a temptation, she just sent Jesus to the door.

Prayer For The Day:

> *Lord Jesus, I need Your power continually.*
> *You know how many times I am tempted.*

·FEBRUARY 9·

> *"I live by the faith*
> *of the Son of God, who loved me,*
> *and gave himself for me."*
>
> *Galatians 2:20*

One day, by a simple act of faith, I decided to take Jesus Christ at His word. I could not come by way of the intellect alone; no one can. That does not mean that we reject reason. God has given us minds and the ability to reason wherever reason is appropriate, but the final and decisive step is taken by faith. I came by faith. Does it work when a person comes, repenting of his sins, to receive Christ by faith? I can only tell you that it worked in my own life. Something did happen to me. I didn't become perfect, but the direction of my life was changed. I found a new dimension to life. I found a new capacity to love that I had never known before.

Prayer For The Day:

The day I received You, Lord, it was
a childlike act of faith. My whole life was changed!

•FEBRUARY 10•

"Our fellowship is with the Father,
and with His Son Jesus Christ."

1 John 1:3

God made you! You were fashioned in His own image! You were made in the image and likeness of the Creator. God had a purpose in making you. His primary purpose was that you would have fellowship with Him. If man does not have fellowship with God, he is lost, confused, and bewildered. Since he does not find his place, he has a sense of not fitting. There are thousands of people who admit and confess that they are unhappy. Economic security, recreation, pleasure, and a good community in which to live have not brought about the peace and happiness that they expected. The reason is that man was created in the image of God and cannot find complete rest, happiness, joy, and peace until he comes back to God.

Prayer For The Day:

Help me this day, Father, to tell others
of the fellowship that can be theirs. Your love will enable me.

•FEBRUARY 11•

". . . that ye may prove
what is that good, and acceptable,
and perfect, will of God."

Romans 12:2

God has a plan for the life of every Christian. Every circumstance, every turn of destiny, is for your good. It is working together for completeness. His plan for you is being perfected. All things working together for your good and for His glory. As a young Christian, Ruth, my wife, wanted to be a missionary, as were her father and mother. But God had other plans for her life. Changing circumstances revealed God's will to her, and she is happy where God has placed her. So many of us ask God to change the circumstances to suit our desires, instead of us conforming our wills to His. Don't let circumstances distress you. Rather, look for the will of God for your life to be revealed in and through those circumstances.

Prayer For The Day:

How often I want to run ahead of Your leading, Father.
Let me trust You completely and realize that in the midst of all
the events of this day, You are working out Your will for my life.

◆FEBRUARY 12◆

"He that loveth his
brother abideth in the light . . ."

1 John 2:10

This age in which we live could hardly be described as conducive to a sensitiveness of the needs of others. We have developed a veneer of sophistication and hardness. Abraham Lincoln once said, characteristically, "I am sorry for the man who can't feel the whip when it is laid on the other man's back." Much of the world is calloused and indifferent toward mankind's poverty and distress. This is due largely to the fact that for many people there has never been a rebirth. The love of God has never been shed abroad in their hearts. Many people speak of the social gospel as though it were separate and apart from the redemptive Gospel. The truth is: there is only one Gospel. We must be redeemed, we must be made right with God before we can become sensitive to the needs of others. Divine love, like a reflected sunbeam, shines down before it radiates out. Unless our hearts are conditioned by the Holy Spirit to receive and reflect the warmth of God's compassion, we cannot love our fellowmen as we ought.

Prayer For The Day:

Help me to feel another person's hurt and be concerned,
Father, so that I may shed the light of Your love
in an uncaring world.

·FEBRUARY 13·

". . . you have been chosen by God
who has given you this new kind of life . . ."
Colossians 3:12 (TLB)

Modern writers depict the pessimism of our time and many of them throw up their hands in despair and say, "There is no answer to man's dilemma." Hemingway once said, "I live in a vacuum that is as lonely as a radio tube when the batteries are dead, and there is no current to plug into." Eugene O'Neill in "Long Day's Journey Into Night" typifies the philosophical attitude of our day. He says, "Life's only meaning is death." I say to Hemingway and to O'Neill, who have already gone on, "There is more to life than death." There is more to life than a radio tube that needs a place to plug into. Jesus taught us the dignity and importance of being a person. God put us on this earth for a purpose, and our purpose is fellowship with God and to glorify God.

Prayer For The Day:

Loving Father, Your love for me transcends the
hopelessness of this life and gives me the purpose I so desperately
need.

Dad's Bday
1909

·FEBRUARY 14·

"I have loved thee
with an everlasting love . . ."
Jeremiah 31:3

No human experience can fully illustrate the imputed righteousness of God, as conceived by His infinite love. It is a mystery—incomprehensible and inexplicable. Like the mystery of the sun's heat and light, we cannot measure it or explain it, and yet we could not live without it. Writing of the mystery of completed righteousness, Paul said, "We speak the wisdom of God in a mystery, even the hidden wisdom, which God ordained before the world unto our glory . . .. But as it is written, Eye hath not seen, nor ear heard, neither have entered into the heart of man, the things which God hath prepared for them that love Him" (1 Corinthians 2:7,9). What God has wrought in us is wonderful. But His work has just begun. He has a wonderful, exciting, thrilling future for all of His believing children.

My finite mind cannot grasp all there is in store
for those of us who love You—but this does not take away
the joy and expectation all Your love has prepared—everlastingly!

◆ FEBRUARY 15 ◆

"Peace I leave with you,
my peace I give unto you . . ."

John 14:27

J esus said, "Blessed are the peacemakers: for they shall be called the children of God." Where does peacemaking begin? How can we become peacemakers? Can peace be discovered within ourselves? Freud has told us that peace is but a mental attitude. Cast off our phobias, shed our neuroses, and "bingo!"—we'll have the coveted peace we long for. I respect psychiatry for what it can do. Unquestionably, it has helped many. But it certainly is not satisfactory as a substitute for the peace which can come only from God. If psychiatry leaves God out, ultimately we shall see psychiatrists going to each other for treatment. There can be no peace until we find peace with God. The Bible says, "He is our peace."

Prayer For The Day:

The balm of Your peace pours over
my soul and I humbly praise You, almighty God.

◆ FEBRUARY 16 ◆

"Good salt is worthless if it
loses its saltiness; it can't season anything.
So don't lose your flavor!"

Mark 9:50 (TLB)

C olumbus was called mad because he decided to sail the uncharted ocean. . . . Martin Luther was called mad because he presumed to defy the entrenched religious hierarchy of his time. Patrick Henry was considered mad when he cried, "Give me liberty, or give me death!" George Washington was thought to be mad when he decided to continue the war after the winter at Valley Forge, when thousands of his men had died and other thousands had deserted, leaving him only a handful of men. We have become too sophisticated and respectable to be called mad in our generation. Christianity has become so respectable and so conventional that it is now insipid. The salt has lost its flavor. . . . Would to God that the world found us Christians dangerous enough to call us mad, in these days when materialism and secularism are sweeping over the world. Thank God there are those who sacrifice time, talents, social position, and lucrative posts, and who fling aside every advantage in order to serve the Kingdom of God.

Prayer For The Day:

Instill in me, Lord Jesus, the same savor
that the disciples showed as they lived so enthusiastically for You.

·FEBRUARY 17·

"I create new heavens . . ."

Isaiah 65:17

What kind of place is Heaven? First, Heaven is home. The Bible takes the word "home" with all of its tender associations and with all of its sacred memories and tells us that Heaven is home. Second, Heaven is a home which is permanent. We have the promise of a home where Christ's followers will remain forever. Third, the Bible teaches that Heaven is a home which is beautiful beyond every imagination. Heaven could not help but be so, because God is a God of beauty. Fourth, the Bible teaches that Heaven will be a home which is happy, because there will be nothing to make it sad. In Heaven families and friends will be reunited. God's house will be a happy home because Christ will be there. He will be the center of Heaven. To Him all hearts will turn, and upon Him all eyes will rest.

Prayer For The Day:

As I think of the promise of an eternal home
with You and the reunion with my loved ones—I rejoice!

•FEBRUARY 18•

"And Jesus said, . . . and ye shall see
the Son of man sitting on the right hand of
power, and coming in the clouds of heaven."

Mark 14:62

The world in which we live is full of pessimism. No Christian has the scriptural right to go around wringing his hands wondering what we are to do in the face of the present world situation. The Scripture says that in the midst of persecution, confusion, wars and rumors of wars, we are to comfort one another with the knowledge that our Lord Jesus Christ is coming back in triumph, glory and majesty. Many times when I go to bed at night I think to myself that before I awaken Christ may come. Sometimes when I get up and look at the dawn I think that perhaps this is the day He will come. He has told us Christians to be watching constantly and to be ready, "for in such an hour as ye think not the Son of man cometh" (Matthew 24:44). Do you think Christ will come today? "Probably not," you say. It is on just such a day that He may come. What a glorious time of reunion it's going to be, when we shall be caught up with Him!

Prayer For The Day:

Thank You, Jesus, for the hope
that even today I may have the joy of seeing You face to face!

•FEBRUARY 19•

"If any man among you seem to be religious,
and bridleth not his tongue, but deceiveth his
own heart, this man's religion is vain."

James 1:26

The problems of the world could be solved overnight if men could get victory over their tongues. Suppose there was no anger, no profanity, no lying, no grumbling or complaining; suppose there were no dirty stories told, no unjust criticism—what a different world this would be! The Bible teaches that a man who can control his tongue can control his whole personality. We should ask ourselves three questions before we speak: Is it true? Is it kind? Does it glorify Christ? If we would always think before we speak, there would be much less evil speaking, and there would soon be a spiritual awakening that would sweep the church in America.

Prayer For The Day:

> *May I remember how important it is to keep a check*
> *on my tongue. I pray that my conversation this day*
> *will be pleasing in Your sight, Lord.*

•FEBRUARY 20•

> *"Thy word have I hid in mine heart,*
> *that I might not sin against thee."*
>
> Psalm 119:11

When temptations come, let me suggest that you ask God for strength—and also to show you the way He has prepared for your escape. One other word of counsel; be very sure that you do not deliberately place yourself in a position to be tempted. All of us are not subjected to the same weaknesses and temptations. To one, alcohol may be the temptation; to another, it may be impure thoughts and acts; to another, greed and covetousness; to another, criticism and an unloving attitude. Regardless of what it may be, be sure that Satan will tempt you at your weak point, not the strong. Our Lord has given us an example of how to overcome the devil's temptations. When He was tempted in the wilderness, He defeated Satan every time by the use of the Bible.

Prayer For The Day:

> *With the shield of Your Word,*
> *I will face temptation, almighty God.*

•FEBRUARY 21•

> *"If any of you lack wisdom, let him*
> *ask of God . . . and it shall be given him."*
>
> James 1:5

Peace with God and the peace of God in a man's heart and the joy of fellowship with Christ have in themselves a beneficial effect upon the body and mind, and will lead to the development and preservation of physical and mental power. Thus, Christ promotes the best interest of the body and mind as well as of the spirit—in addition to inward peace, the development of spiritual life, the joy and fellowship with Christ, and the new strength that come with being born again. There are certain special privileges that only the true Christian can enjoy. There is, for example, the privilege of having divine wisdom and guidance continually.

Prayer For The Day:

> *Let me live so close to You, almighty God,*
> *that Your wisdom will invade my mind continually.*

·FEBRUARY 22·

> *"In every battle you will need faith*
> *as your shield to stop the fiery arrows*
> *aimed at you by Satan."*
> *Ephesians 6:16 (TLB)*

Many jokes are made about the devil, but the devil is no joke. If a short time ago I had talked about Satan to university students, they would have made light of him, but no longer. Students today want to know about the devil, about witchcraft, about the occult. Many people do not know they are turning to Satan. They are being deluded because, according to Jesus Christ, Satan is the father of lies and the greatest liar of all times. He is called a deceiver. In order to accomplish his purpose, the devil blinds people to their need of Christ. Two forces are at work in our world— the forces of Christ and the forces of the devil—and you are asked to choose.

Prayer For The Day:

> *I have chosen to serve You, my Lord Jesus.*
> *Give me Your strength to battle the deceptions of Satan.*

·FEBRUARY 23·

> *"I can do all things*
> *through Christ which strengtheneth me."*
> *Philippians 4:13*

Jesus had a humble heart. If He abides in us, pride will never dominate our lives. Jesus had a loving heart. If He dwells within us, hatred and bitterness will never rule us. Jesus had a forgiving and understanding heart. If He lives within us, mercy will temper our relationships with our fellowmen. Jesus had an unselfish heart. If He lives in us, selfishness will not predominate, but service to God and others will come before our selfish interests. You say, "That's a big order!" I admit that. It would be impossible if you had to measure up to Him in your own strength and with your natural heart. Paul recognized that he could never attain this heart purity by his own striving.

Prayer For The Day:

> So live in me today that I will be
> able to radiate Your love and grace, Jesus.

•FEBRUARY 24•

"Who is a God like unto thee . . .
he delighteth in mercy."

Micah 7:18

Danny died today in 2006

M any persons want to hear what God says just out of curiousity. They want to analyze and dissect it in their own test tubes. To these persons, God may remain the great cosmic silence "out there somewhere." He communicates to those who are willing to hear and receive Him, and willing to obey Him. Jesus said that we must become humble as little children, and God has most often revealed Himself to the meek and the humble—to a shepherd boy like David, to a rough desert man like John the Baptist, to shepherds watching their flocks, to a girl named Mary. How does God speak? How can a blind man see? How can a deaf man hear? From the beginning God spoke to man. Adam heard the voice of the Lord in the Garden of Eden. Adam had two sons, Cain and Abel, and God spoke to them. Cain spurned that which was revealed to him, but Abel was obedient to the Word of God. Abel's response showed that a man tainted and handicapped by sin could respond to God's overtures. Thus, in the beginning, God began by revelation to build a bridge between Himself and people.

Prayer For The Day:

> How merciful You are,
> almighty God. I seek to show this same mercy.

·FEBRUARY 25·

"Christ taught you!
If you have really heard his voice . . .
then throw off your old evil nature—the old you
that was a partner in your evil ways . . ."
Ephesians 4:20-22 (TLB)

P aul before his conversion was not meek. Proudly and bru-
tally, he apprehended all Christians and sought to destroy
them. He was bigoted, selfish, and vaunted. But when he wrote his
warm and affectionate letter to the churches of Galatia, he said,
among other things, "The fruit of the Spirit is . . . gentleness, goodness . . . meekness." His meekness was something God-given, not
something man-made. It is not our nature to be meek. On the contrary, it is our nature to be proud and haughty. That is why the
new birth is so essential to each of us. That is why Jesus frankly and
pointedly said not only to Nicodemus but to every one of us, "Ye
must be born again." Meekness begins there! You must have a
change of nature.

Prayer For The Day:

Heavenly Father, give me
the same kind of meekness that You gave to Jesus.

·FEBRUARY 26·

"But when the Holy Spirit controls our lives
he will produce this kind of fruit in us: love, joy,
peace, patience, kindness, goodness,
faithfulness, gentleness and self-control . . ."
Galatians 5:22,23 (TLB)

C hrist can rid you of inner conflict. Man without God is always torn between two urges. His nature prompts him to do
wrong, and his conscience urges him to do right. Antagonistic desires and crossed-up emotions keep him in a state of personal insta-
bility. Medical men have almost concluded that this conflict is the
basis of much physical breakdown and nervous collapse. Many
doctors now believe that among the contributing causes of the common cold are stress, tension, and inner conflict. Paul must have
been in the midst of such a personal civil war when he cried, "O
wretched man that I am! Who shall deliver me from the body of

this death?" Then he answered his own question when he said, "I thank God through Jesus Christ our Lord."

Prayer For The Day:

Only Your Holy Spirit, Lord, can control my innermost feelings. Help me to be conscious of Your presence this day.

D'o Bday 1909

•FEBRUARY 27•

"Because I live, ye shall live also."
John 14:19

For personal Christianity, the resurrection is all-important. There is a vital interrelation to the existence of Christianity itself, as well as to the individual believer, in the message of the Gospel. The Swiss theologian, Karl Barth, said, "Do you want to believe in the living Christ? We may believe in Him only if we believe in His corporeal resurrection. This is the content of the New Testament. We are always free to reject it, but not to modify it, nor to pretend that the New Testament tells something else. We may accept or refuse the message, but we may not change it." Christianity as a system of truth collapses if the resurrection is rejected. That Jesus rose from the dead is one of the foundation stones of our faith.

Prayer For The Day:

Lord, let me live today with the constant thought that You are alive!

•FEBRUARY 28•

"These things have I written unto you that believe . . . that ye may know that ye have eternal life . . ."
1 John 5:13

Recently I read that it will cost this country a hundred billion dollars to get one man safely to Mars. It cost God the priceless blood of His only Son to get us sinners to heaven. By tasting death for every man, Jesus took over our penalty as He erased our guilt. Now God can forgive. In a moment of thanksgiving, Paul once exclaimed, "He loved me and gave Himself for me!" Will you repeat these words right now, even as you read? If you do, I believe you will have cause to be thankful too, and that you will experience the love of God in your heart. Try it and see. The Bible teaches that you can be absolutely sure that you are saved.

Prayer For The Day:

Father, although my finite mind
cannot understand all the wonders of the Gospel,
I thank You for the assurance of my salvation through Christ.

•FEBRUARY 29•

". . . for the Lord thy God,
he it is that doth go with thee;
he will not fail thee, nor forsake thee."
                                        Deuteronomy 31:6

Loneliness is no respecter of persons. It invades the palace as well as the hut. Many turn to drink because of loneliness. Others lose their sanity because of loneliness. Many commit suicide because of the despair of loneliness. Thousands have found Christ to be the answer for their loneliness. The Hebrew children were not alone when they were hurled into the fiery furnace of persecution. There was One with them like unto the Son of God. Moses wasn't alone in the Midian Desert when God came to comfort him and call him to a wider ministry. Elijah wasn't alone at the cave when God came near and spoke with the still, small voice. Paul and Silas were not alone in the Philippian jail when God came down and gave them a song at midnight. Whoever you are, Christ can give you comfort and companionship.

Prayer For The Day:

Whenever I begin to feel alone, help me
remember that You are always with me. Sometimes
the way seems dark but You are still there. Thank You, Lord.

•MARCH 1•

*"How can a young man stay pure? By
reading your word and following its rules."*
Psalm 119:9

Many of the difficulties we experience as Christians can be
traced to a lack of Bible study and reading. We should not
be content to skim through a chapter merely to satisfy our conscience. Hide the Word of God in your heart! A little portion well
digested is of greater value to the soul than a lengthy portion
scanned hurriedly. Do not be discouraged because you cannot understand it all. Go on reading. As you read, the Holy Spirit will
enlighten the passages for you. Reading the Bible has a purifying
effect upon the heart and mind.

Prayer For The Day:

*Let the enlightenment of the riches
of Your Word sink deep within my soul, Lord.*

•MARCH 2•

*"You deserve honesty from
the heart; yes, utter sincerity and
truthfulness. Oh, give me this wisdom."*
Psalm 51:6 (TLB)

The Bible teaches that purity of conduct includes truthfulness.
The Bible teaches that we should be truthful in our represen-
tation of ourselves. With what scorn Christ denounced the hypocrisy of the scribes and Pharisees! In the Sermon on the Mount He
rebuked all hypocritical giving, praying, and fasting. We should
also be truthful in speaking of our past achievements in our particular vocation. God does not ask us to understate the facts—that
might even be untruthfulness—but neither does He want us to
overrate our achievements or our gifts, either in thought or in
speech. A lie is anything contrary to the naked truth.

Prayer For The Day:

*It is so easy, Lord, to embellish the truth.
Give me Your wisdom to be
completely honest in every phase of my life.*

·MARCH 3·

*"He made the world
and everything there is."*

Hebrews 1:2

There are many arguments we could marshal to give evidence of the existence of God. There is scientific evidence pointing to God's existence. For example, whatever is in motion must be moved by another, for motion is the response of matter to power. In the world of matter there can be no power without life, and life pre-supposes a being from which emanates the power to move things, such as tides and the planets. Or there is the argument that says nothing can be the cause of itself. It would be prior to itself if it caused itself to be, and that is an absurdity. Then there is the law of life. We see objects that have no intellect, such as stars and planets, moving in a consistent pattern, cooperating ingeniously with one another. Hence, it is evident that they achieve their movements not by accident but by design. Whatever lacks intelligence cannot move intelligently. An arrow would be useless without a bow and an archer. What gives direction and purpose and design to inanimate objects? It is God. He is the underlying, motivating force of life.

Prayer For The Day:

*Lord, I know that without Your power
my life would be useless. Prompt me,
by Your Holy Spirit, to glorify You in everything I do.*

·MARCH 4·

*"But don't forget this, dear friends. . . . He isn't
really being slow about his promised return,
even though it sometimes seems that way.
But he is waiting, for the good reason that he is
not willing that any should perish, and he is
giving more time for sinners to repent."*

2 Peter 3:8,9 (TLB)

Many people are asking, "Where is history heading?" A careful student of the Bible will be led to see that God controls the clock of destiny. Amid the world's confusion, God's omnipotent hand moves, working out His unchanging plan and purpose.

The Communists say that time and history are on their side. But they are ignorant of the fact that Jesus Christ is coming to earth again. It is Christ who is in control, and He will determine the outcome. George Whitefield, the great English evangelist, said, "I am daily waiting for the coming of the Son of God." But he did not sit down and do nothing. He burned out his life in proclaiming the Gospel of Christ.

Prayer For The Day:

Father, deliver me from slothfulness, keep me
quickened to deliver Your message of salvation to
everyone who will listen, until that day I die or You return again.

◆MARCH 5◆

"So he went and did
according unto the word of the Lord . . ."
1 Kings 17:5

A s messengers of God, we will often lead lonely lives. "All men forsook me," said Paul. It is a price we have to pay; there is a loneliness in the Gospel. Yet you will not be alone, because you will be ministered to by the Spirit of God, as Elijah was ministered to at the brook Cherith. A true messenger lives a burdened life. If he is the Lord's vessel, he carries in his heart a burden for souls none can share but those who know it firsthand

Prayer For The Day:

Just as Your Spirit took care of Elijah,
I know I am not alone in Your service, almighty God.

◆MARCH 6◆

"If thou shalt confess with thy mouth the
Lord Jesus, and shalt believe in thine heart
that God hath raised him from the dead,
thou shalt be saved."
Romans 10:9

T he heart is the blood-pump of the body. It is also used metaphorically when we speak of affections and feelings. Since it is the central organ of the body and one of the most vital, the Bible speaks of it as the wellspring of life. Hence, it is used synonymously with "life." When the Bible says, "Son, give me thine heart," it doesn't mean that we are to cut out our actual hearts and give them to God. It means that we are to give Him our lives, our all. When we come to Christ, we are not only to give intellectual assent with our minds, we are to "believe in our hearts." We can believe in the historic Jesus, but if we have "saving faith" our belief must involve our whole being. When we believe with all our hearts, the will, the emotions, and the intellect are surrendered to Christ.

Prayer For The Day:

Lord, I believe and rejoice in
the knowledge that You are alive and my Redeemer!

·MARCH 7·

"For salvation that comes from
trusting Christ . . . is already within easy
reach of each of us . . ."
Romans 10:8 (TLB)

C hrist said there is a happiness in that acknowledgment of spiritual poverty which lets God come into our souls. Now, the Bible teaches that our souls have a disease. It causes all the troubles and difficulties in the world. It causes all the troubles, confusions, and disillusionments in your own life. The name of the disease is an ugly word. We don't like to use it. It is "sin." All of us have pride. We do not like to confess that we are wrong or that we have failed. But God says, "All have sinned and come short of the glory of God." We have failed to live up to the divine standard. We must confess our sin as the first step to happiness, peace, and contentment.

Prayer For The Day:

Pride kept me so long
from acknowledging my need of You, Lord.
Each day, help me to realize I am nothing without You.

·MARCH 8·

*"Stop loving this evil world and all
that it offers you, for when you love these things
you show that you do not really love God . . ."*
1 John 2:15 (TLB)

There are certain elements of daily life which are not sinful in themselves but which have a tendency to lead to sin if they are abused. Abuse literally means "extreme use" and, in many instances, overuse of things lawful becomes sin. Ambition is an essential part of character, but it must be fixed on lawful objects and exercised in proper proportion. Thought about the necessities of life and taking care of one's family is absolutely essential; but this can degenerate into anxiety, and then, as Christ reminded us, the cares of this life choke the spiritual seed in the heart. Making of money is essential for daily living; but money-making is apt to degenerate into money-loving, and then the deceitfulness of riches enters and spoils our spiritual life. Much so-called worldliness in Christian circles is misunderstood. You cannot confine it to a particular rank, walk or circumstance of life, and say that one person is spiritual and another is unspiritual. Worldliness is actually a spirit, an atmosphere, an influence permeating the whole of life and human society, and it needs to be guarded against constantly and strenuously.

Prayer For The Day:

*Lord, keep me sensitive to Your Spirit that
I may not fall into the spirit of worldliness and its lusts.*

·MARCH 9·

"That Christ may dwell in your hearts by faith . . ."
Ephesians 3:17

Experts have told us that society is sick. Their panaceas have treated human frailty with infusions of low-income housing, welfare payments, integrated education, and psychological conditioning. But we are learning that this is not the total answer. The world does need changing, society needs changing, the nation needs changing, but we never will change it until we ourselves are changed. And we never will change until we look into the mirror of our own soul and face with candor what we are inside. Then freely acknowledge that there is a defect in human nature, a built-in waywardness that comes from man's natural rebellion against God. I am not preaching now, just trying to give you an understanding of what makes you tick. But I also expect to show you that, in the end, you can find your answers only in a personal relationship with God.

Prayer For The Day:

It is useless to hide the real me from You.
I pour out this day, all my innermost thoughts and feelings,
Lord Jesus.

•MARCH 10•

"... not having mine own righteousness ..."
Philippians 3:9

People go through many doors which do not lead to the Kingdom of God. Some try the door of good works. They say, "I can get to heaven if I only do enough good things, because God will honor all the good things I do." It's wonderful to do good things, but we cannot do enough good things to satisfy God. God demands perfection, and we're not perfect. If we're going to enter the Kingdom of Heaven, we have to be absolutely perfect. You ask, "Well, how will I ever be perfect?" We need to be clothed in the righteousness of the Lord Jesus. There is one door to the Kingdom and it's Jesus. And we will never get to heaven unless we go His way.

Prayer For The Day:

Almighty God, there is nothing
I can do to be worthy of Your love,
and yet You have given me Jesus—my Savior and Lord!

•MARCH 11•

"Submit yourselves therefore to God ..."
James 4:7

You have a tongue and a voice. These instruments of speech can be used destructively or employed constructively. You can use your tongue to slander, to gripe, to scold, to nag, and to quarrel; or you can bring it under the control of God's Spirit and make it an instrument of blessing and praise. The 20th-century version of James 3:3 says, "When we put bits into the horses' mouths to make them obey us, we control the rest of their bodies also." Just so, when we submit to the claims of Christ upon our lives, our untamed natures are brought under His control. We become meek, tamed, and "fit for the Master's service."

Prayer For The Day:

> *I would be under Your control, Lord Jesus Christ.*
> *Take away the pride that keeps me from complete submission.*

·MARCH 12·

> *"Dear brothers, I have been*
> *talking to you as though you were still just*
> *babies in the Christian life . . ."*
> *1 Corinthians 3:1 (TLB)*

Some people have received Christ but have never reached spiritual maturity. They have been in church all their lives, and yet they have never become mature Christians. They are still considered "spiritual children" and "babes in Christ." They know little Scripture. They have little desire to pray, and bear few of the marks of a Christian in their daily living. To say, "I will resolve to do better, I will muster all my will power and revise my way of living," is noble, but futile. A corpse could as well say, "I will—through sheer effort—rise out of this coffin and be a living man again." You need a power outside yourself. You cannot get over the habits and chains that are binding you. You need outside help. You need Christ. The Bible tells of a bridge of faith which reaches from the valley of despair to the high hills of glorious hope in Christ. It tells where we are, but beyond that—it tells where we may be in Christ. Now, of course, you will not be completely mature until you are in the presence of Christ, but you should be growing every day as a Christian.

Prayer For The Day:

> *Lord, work through me this day,*
> *that I might be maturing as a Christian and*
> *come to know You better, that I might know*
> *Your perfect will for me.*

·MARCH 13·

*"The Lord is my rock,
and my fortress, and my deliverer; my God,
my strength, in whom I will trust . . ."*

Psalm 18:2

The trouble with our modern thinking is that we have a conception that God is a haphazard God with no set rules of life and salvation. Ask the astronomer if God is a haphazard God. He will tell you that every star moves with precision in its celestial path. Ask the scientist if God is a haphazard God. He will tell you that His formulas and equations are fixed, and that to ignore the laws of science would be a fool's folly. If the laws in the material realm are so fixed and exact, is it reasonable that God could afford to be haphazard in the spiritual realm where eternal destinies of souls are at stake? Just as God has equations and rules in the material realm, God has equations and rules in the spiritual.

Prayer For The Day:

*Thank You, God, for Your absolute divine order.
Amid confusion, it brings me hope and perfect peace.*

·MARCH 14·

*"So don't be anxious about tomorrow.
God will take care of your tomorrow too.
Live one day at a time."*

Matthew 6:34 (TLB)

King George V wrote on the flyleaf of the Bible of a friend, "The secret of happiness is not to do what you like to do, but to learn to like what you have to do." Too many think of happiness as some sort of will-o'-the-wisp thing that is discovered by constant and relentless searching. It is not found by seeking. It is not an end in itself. Pots of gold are never found at the end of the rainbow, as we used to think when we were children; gold is mined from the ground or panned laboriously from a mountain stream. Jesus once told His disciples, "Seek ye first the kingdom of God, and his righteousness, and all these things shall be added unto you." The "things" He spoke of were the things that make us feel happy and secure—food, drink, clothes, shelter. He told us not to make these the chief goal of our lives but to "seek the kingdom" and these needs would be automatically supplied. There, if we will take it, is the secret of happiness.

Prayer For The Day:

*Forgive me, Father, for the times when
I am anxious. You have promised to take care of all my needs.*

·MARCH 15·

*". . . may the God of peace . . .
produce in you through the power of Christ
all that is pleasing to him . . ."*
Hebrews 13:20,21 (TLB)

When I was a boy, radio was just coming of age. We would gather around a crude homemade set and twist the three tuning dials in an effort to establish contact with the transmitter. Often, all the sound that came out of the amplifier was the squawk of static; but we knew that somewhere out there was the unseen transmitter, and if contact was established and the dials were in adjustment, we could hear a voice loud and clear. After a long time of laborious tuning, the far distant voice would suddenly break through and a smile of triumph would illuminate the faces of all in the room. At last we were tuned in! In the revelation that God established between Himself and us, we can find a new life and a new dimension of living, but we must "tune in." There are higher levels of living to which we have never attained. There is peace, satisfaction, and joy that we have never experienced. God is trying to break through to us. The heavens are calling. God is speaking! Let man hear.

Prayer For The Day:

*Lord, help me to be so attuned to Your will that
I will experience all that You so lovingly wish to bestow.*

·MARCH 16·

"I pray that you will begin to understand
how incredibly great his power is to help those
who believe him. It is that same mighty power
that raised Christ from the dead . . ."

Ephesians 1:19,20 (TLB)

J esus told His disciples that the world would hate them. They would be "as sheep in the midst of wolves." They would be arrested, scourged, and brought before governors and kings. Even their loved ones would persecute them. As the world hated and persecuted Him, so it would treat His servants. Thousands of Christians have learned the secret of contentment and joy in trial. Some of the happiest Christians I have met have been life-long sufferers. They have had every reason to sigh and complain, being denied so many privileges and pleasures that they see others enjoy, yet they have found greater cause for gratitude and joy than many who are prosperous, vigorous, and strong. In all ages, Christians have found it possible to maintain the spirit of joy in the hour of trial. In circumstances that would have felled most men, they have so completely risen above them that they actually have used the circumstances to serve and glorify Christ.

Prayer For The Day:

Lord Jesus, keep us ever mindful of the need
to rejoice in You constantly; to go beyond the circumstance,
no matter how desperate, and to see You as our hope and joy.

·MARCH 17·

". . . one thing I know, that,
whereas I was blind, now I see."

John 9:25

I try to explain to you the joy of following Christ: the thrill, the excitement, the exhilaration—knowing where I've come from, why I'm here, where I'm going! There's a reason for existence. There's a reason for getting up every morning of the year. I try to tell you what I've found in Jesus Christ, and in studying the Scriptures and walking with Him, and you say, "I can't see that!" Of course, you can't. You are blind. Try to explain television to a blind man. He can understand a little of it, but it doesn't make sense to him. Try to explain a sunset to him. He's blind to it. The scales must be removed from your eyes, and only Christ can do that. He can remove them right now and you can start living and seeing a whole new world that you never knew existed, if you will let Him open your spiritual eyes.

Prayer For The Day:

*I thank You for that Power that
is able to give sight to the spiritually
blinded eyes of each person who trusts in You, Lord Jesus.*

⋆MARCH 18⋆

"Doest thou well to be angry?"

Jonah 4:4

Y ou have a temper! There is nothing unique about that. Most people have tempers, in varying degrees, of course. God does not ask that you get rid of that temper. But He does say that if you are to be happy, it must be brought under control and rechanneled to proper use. God cannot use a man without a temper as well as one with a controlled temper. Too many professed Christians never get "wrought up" about anything; they never get indignant with injustice, with corruption in high places, or with the godless traffics which barter away the souls and bodies of men.

Prayer For The Day:

*Use my anger to help others, Lord.
When I see them hurting or Your world decaying,
let me be challenged to reach out—instead of merely exploding.*

⋆MARCH 19⋆

*"And Jesus answering saith
unto them, Have faith in God."*

Mark 11:22

D r. Wernher von Braun, the guiding scientist in the development of our great space rockets, has said, "The materialists of the 19th century and the Marxist heirs of the 20th tried to tell us that as science yields more knowledge about the creation, it makes us able to live without faith in a Creator. Yet so far, with every new answer we have discovered new questions. The better we understand the intricacies of the atomic structure, the nature of life and the master plan for the galaxies, the more reason we have found to marvel at the wonder of God's creation. But our need for God is not based on awe alone. Man needs faith just as he needs food, water and air. With all the science in the world, we need faith in God."

Prayer For The Day:

Father, man's incredible inventions are so insignificant when I contemplate Your magnificent creation. Yet, in complete dependence, I realize my need of faith in You for my smallest need.

·MARCH 20·

"So use every piece of God's armor to resist the enemy whenever he attacks, and when it is all over, you will still be standing up."
Ephesians 6:13 (TLB)

Daniel and his companions were tempted to forsake their godly heritage but they refused. They even faced a fiery furnace rather than compromise. God honored their faith and mightily used them. Moses was surrounded by the luxury and godlessness of the Egyptian court, but cast in his lot with his own people. Lot lived in Sodom and saw the obscenities of that doomed city. God saved him out of it because he trusted in Him. Every one of our Lord's apostles sealed their faith with their lives. Since then, history has been replete with the lives of men who have put God and His way of life above all else.

Prayer For The Day:

Help me to stand by faith in You, when I am tempted, almighty God.

·MARCH 21·

"I shall be satisfied,
when I awake, with thy likeness."

Psalm 17:15

I s it not logical to believe that the only one who can recreate us is the One who created us in the first place? If your watch were out of order, you wouldn't take it to a blacksmith. If your car needed overhauling, you wouldn't go to a machine shop. Our spiritual problems can be solved only by the God who created us originally. He created us in His own image and likeness; today, by the grace of His Son, He can recreate us in the likeness of His resurrection. Through faith in Jesus Christ, we are recreated and become partakers of His life.

Prayer For The Day:

There is so much that is out
of order in my life, Lord. Remake all
the parts that need the infinite healing of your re-creation.

·MARCH 22·

"Keep thyself pure."

1 Timothy 5:22

T he Pharisees were not happy men. They had furrowed brows, nervous tension, frustration. They were full of resentments, bitterness, prejudices, and hatreds. Why? Simply because they had lost sight of God's conception of the pure in heart. They thought that as long as they kept the letter of the law that was enough. But this was not God's plan. This did not produce purity of heart. This did not bring about happiness of soul. Jesus taught that God looks deeper than the outside actions of an individual. He searches and ponders the heart. God judges not so much the outside as He does the inside. He looks to the motives, thoughts and intents of your heart.

Prayer For The Day:

Father, give me purity of heart that
in true humility I may serve and praise You.

• MARCH 23 •

*"Jesus Christ the same
yesterday, and today, and for ever."*
Hebrews 13:8

T he Bible says, "It is appointed unto men once to die," and to
the average person this seems a stark and hopeless situation.
Hundreds of philosophies and scores of religions have been in-
vented to circumvent the Word of God. Modern philosophers and
psychologists are still trying to make it appear that there is some
way out other than the path of Jesus. But people have tried them
all, and none of them leads anywhere but down. Christ came to
give us the answers to the three enduring problems of sin, sorrow,
and death. It is Jesus Christ, and He alone, who is also enduring
and unchanging, "the same yesterday, today and forever." All
other things may change, but Christ remains unchangeable. In the
restless sea of human passions Christ stands steadfast and calm,
ready to welcome all who will turn to Him and accept the blessings
of safety and peace. For we are living in an age of grace, in which
God promises that "whosoever will" may come and receive His
Son. But this period of grace will not go on indefinitely. We are
even now living on borrowed time.

Prayer For The Day:

*Jesus, even if loved ones
friends, acquaintances change, You are
always the same. Thank You for Your unchanging love.*

• MARCH 24 •

*"But to all who received him,
he gave the right to become children of God."*
John 1:12 (TLB)

W ho can describe or measure the love of God? God is love.
But the fact that God is love does not mean that everything
is sweet, beautiful, and happy, and that God's love could not possibly allow punishment for sin. God's holiness demands that all sin
be punished, but God's love provided a plan of redemption and
salvation for sinful man. God's love provided the cross of Jesus
Christ by which man can have forgiveness and cleansing. It was the
love of God that sent Jesus Christ to the cross. No matter what sin

you have committed, no matter how black, dirty, shameful, or terrible it may be, God loves you. Yet this love of God that is immeasurable, unmistakable, and unending, this love of God that reaches to wherever a man is, can be entirely rejected. God will not force Himself upon anyone against his will. It is your part to believe. It is your part to receive. Nobody else can do it for you.

Prayer For The Day:

Your love overwhelms me, Father.
In spite of my sin, Jesus' death on the cross
can cleanse me from all the past. Humbly I accept this gift, Lord.

·MARCH 25·

"If a person isn't loving and kind,
it shows that he doesn't know God—
for God is love."

1 John 4:8 (TLB)

J esus wept tears of compassion at the graveside of a friend. He mourned over Jerusalem because as a city it had lost its appreciation of the things of the Spirit. His great heart was sensitive to the needs of others. To emphasize the importance of man's love for men, He revised an old commandment to make it read, "Thou shalt love the Lord thy God with all thy heart . . . and thy neighbor as thyself." This generation is rough and tough. I heard a little boy boasting one day about how tough he was. He said, "On the street I live on, the farther out you go the tougher they get, and I live in the last house." Until you have learned the value of compassionately sharing others' sorrow, distress, and misfortune, you cannot know real happiness.

Prayer For The Day:

Lord Jesus, sensitize my heart
with Your compassion so that I may truly love.

·MARCH 26·

T&C Married this day in 1960 (handwritten margin note)

*". . . light is come into the world, and
men loved darkness rather than light . . ."*
John 3:19

The world's difficulty is summed up in the words, "And the light shineth in darkness; and the darkness understood it not." The light of Easter is shining, but men refuse to turn to its healing rays for forgiveness, redemption and salvation. Thus Christ is being rejected by the overwhelming majority of humanity today. As a result, men stumble on in spiritual darkness blindly toward destruction, judgment, and hell. In the midst of the darkness and "void" at the creation of the world, God said, "Let there be light." In your own mind-darkened, will-paralyzed, conscience-dulled soul, God can make the light penetrate and turn the darkness of your own life into day, if you will let Him. Many of you are living in spiritual darkness; confused, frustrated, disturbed and fearful. Let the Light come into your heart by faith.

Prayer For The Day:

*At Easter time, as nature breaks through into
glorious re-creation, I am reminded of the glory of
Your resurrection! I praise You, Lord Jesus,
for Your light which shines through the dimness of my soul.*

·MARCH 27·

*". . . he that shall humble
himself shall be exalted."*
Matthew 23:12

In almost every instance in the Bible, as well as in life, pride is associated with failure, not success. We hear a great deal about the inferiority complex, but the superiority complex of pride is seldom spoken of. It was pride that caused the fall of Lucifer, and he became Satan, the devil. It was pride that led King Saul down to a shameful and untimely death. It was pride that caused Peter to deny his Lord. The greatest act of humility in the history of the universe was when Jesus Christ stooped to die on the cross of Calvary. And before any man can get to heaven, he must kneel at the foot of the cross and acknowledge that he is a sinner, that he has broken the Ten Commandments of God, and that he needs the grace of God in Christ. No man can come proudly to the Savior.

Prayer For The Day:

Lord Jesus, You suffered such humiliation
and pain for me on the cross. I ask You, humbly,
to forgive my pride and errant ways that nailed You there.

•MARCH 28•

"The Lord is my light and my salvation . . ."
Psalm 27:1

Under the picture of Peter Milne, hanging in the church he founded on the little New Hebrides Island of Nguna, these words are found: "When he came, there was no light. When he died, there was no darkness." When Christ came into the world, there was no light. Matthew (quoting Isaiah) said of Him, "The people which sat in darkness saw great light; and to them which sat in the region and shadow of death light is sprung up" (Matthew 4:16). Harry Lauder once said that during his boyhood, he could tell where the lamplighter was "by the trail of light he left behind him." Christ was the heavenly Lamplighter. Everywhere He went, the midnight gloom of sin and despair disappeared before Him.

Prayer For The Day:

My heart and soul praises You,
my risen Redeemer, for the light that
pervades the deepest gloom and transforms our lives with Your
love.

•MARCH 29•

". . . unto him that loved us, and
washed us from our sins in his own blood."
Revelation 1:5

Blood is mentioned 460 times in the Bible. Fourteen times in the New Testament Jesus spoke of His own blood. Why? Because by the shedding of His blood, He accomplished the possibility of our salvation. He paid the penalty for our sin and redeemed us. The penalty for our sin and rebellion is death; Jesus stepped out and said, "I'll take that death." He voluntarily laid down His life and took the penalty we deserve. That's what the cross is all about. The blood of Jesus Christ not only redeems us, it justifies us. Being justified means more than being forgiven. I can say, "I forgive you," but I can't justify you. But God not only forgives the past, He clothes you in righteousness as though you had never committed a sin. Yet it cost the blood of His Son on the cross.

Prayer For The Day:

Lord Jesus, with a deeply grateful heart
I thank You for Your sacrifice upon the cross.
Your blood has cleansed my sin and made me worthy
of forgiveness.

•MARCH 30•

"For God hath not appointed
us to wrath, but to obtain salvation by our
Lord Jesus Christ, who died for us . . ."
1 Thessalonians 5:9,10

Look at Christ's death. In one biography of the great American, Daniel Webster, 863 pages deal with his career and just five pages are devoted to his death. In Hay's life of Abraham Lincoln there are 5,000 pages but only 25 are devoted to the dramatic story of his assassination and death. In most biographies the deaths of the subjects are mere incidents at the close of the books. But when we come to the four "biographies" of Jesus, the four Gospels, we are confronted with a strange fact. One-third of Matthew is given to a description of the death of Christ. One-third of Mark, one-fourth of Luke, and one-half of John are given to His death. All these pages are devoted to the last 24 hours of His life. The death of Jesus Christ is a significant fact in human history, because Jesus Christ came for the express purpose of dying for sinners. When He left heaven, He knew He was going to the cross.

Prayer For The Day:

Lord Jesus, what agony You suffered for me
upon the cross. I deserve Your judgment, yet You have
given me forgiveness and eternal life. I praise Your beloved name.

·MARCH 31·

". . . believe in thine heart that
God hath raised him from the dead . . ."
Romans 10:9

I t is impossible to believe anything into existence. The Gospel did not come into being because men believed it. The tomb was not emptied of Christ's body that first Easter because some faithful persons believed it. The fact preceded the faith. We are psychologically incapable of believing without an object of our faith. The object of Christian faith is Christ. Faith means more than an intellectual assent to the claims of Christ. You are not called upon to believe something that is not credible, but to believe in the fact of history that in reality transcends all history. Faith actually means surrender and commitment to the claims of Christ. We do not know Christ through the five physical senses, but we know Him through the sixth sense that God has given every man—the ability to believe.

Prayer For The Day:

As I keep my eyes on You, Lord, my faith does
not waver. Too often I look down and stumble. Let me
comprehend today afresh the power that raised You from the dead.

·APRIL 1·

"As for me, God forbid that
I should boast about anything except the
cross of our Lord Jesus Christ."
Galatians 6:14 (TLB)

W hat glory is there in the cross? It was an instrument of torture and shame. Why did Paul glory in it? He gloried in it because the most selfless act ever performed by men or angels took place upon it. He saw—emanating from that rough, unartistic beam upon which the Son of God had been crucified—the radiant hope of the world, the end of the believer's bondage to sin, and the love of God shed abroad in the hearts of men. A lone man dying on a cross did more to restore man's lost harmony with God, his fellowman, and himself, than the combined genius and power of earth's mighty. With my finite limitations, I cannot fully comprehend the mystery of Christ's atonement. I only know that all who come to the cross in simple, trusting faith lose all their guilty stains and find peace with God.

Prayer For The Day:

> *Like the Apostle Paul, Father, help me*
> *to glory in the cross of Jesus and more*
> *fully understand the tremendous meaning it has*
> *for me as a believer and for all who would come*
> *to its foot and kneel.*

• APRIL 2 •

> *"And thou shalt love the Lord thy God*
> *with all thy heart, and with all thy soul,*
> *and with all thy mind . . ."*
>
> *Mark 12:30*

C hrist touches every area of our lives. He touches our minds and we are transformed by the renewing of our minds. God invites people to use their minds, "Come now, and let us reason together, saith the Lord" (Isaiah 1:18). We are told in Scripture not to be like the horse or mule, "which have no understanding" (Psalm 32:9). Christ declared that we are to love the Lord our God with all our heart, soul, strength, and mind. We are told to fear God, to love Christ, and to hate sin. Fear, love, and hate are emotions. Dr. Leslie Weatherhead, preaching at the City Temple in London, said, "What is wrong with emotion? Christianity is falling in love with Christ. Has anyone ever fallen in love without emotion?"

Prayer For The Day:

> *May my love for You embrace*
> *my whole being, Lord Jesus. Teach me true love.*

• APRIL 3 •

> *"And he is before all things,*
> *and by him all things consist."*
>
> *Colossians 1:17*

N apoleon was right when he said, "I know men, and I tell you, Jesus is more than a man. Comparison is impossible between Him and any other human being who ever lived, because He was the Son of God." Emerson was right when he replied to those who asked him why he did not include Jesus among his *Representative Men,* "Jesus was not just a man." Arnold Toynbee was right when he said, "As we stand and gaze with our eyes fixed upon the farther shore, a simple figure rises from the flood and straightway fills the whole horizon of history. There is the Savior."

Prayer For The Day:

> *My Savior, I worship and revere Your name*
> *for You are the risen Christ, beloved Son of God.*

⋅APRIL 4⋅

> *"The Lord is close to those*
> *whose hearts are breaking; he rescues those*
> *who are humbly sorry for their sins."*
> *Psalm 34:18 (TLB)*

In God's economy, you must go down into the valley of grief before you can scale the heights of spiritual glory. You must become tired and weary of living alone before you seek and find the fellowship of Christ. You must come to the end of self before you begin to live. The mourning of inadequacy is a weeping that catches the attention of God. The Bible says, "The Lord is nigh unto them that are of a broken heart; and saveth such as be of a contrite spirit." The happiest day of my life was when I realized that my own ability, my own goodness, and my own morality was insufficient in the sight of God; and I publicly and openly acknowledged my need of Christ. I am not exaggerating when I say that my mourning was turned to joy, and my sighing into singing.

Prayer For The Day:

> *In the valleys I have been*
> *drawn closer to You, my God and Comforter.*

·APRIL 5·

"It was written long ago that
the Messiah must suffer and die and rise again
from the dead on the third day."

Luke 24:46 (TLB)

What was the power and influence that changed the cross from an instrument of bloody torture into the most glorious and beloved of all symbols? The Romans had crucified thousands of people before and after Calvary. If Jesus had not risen from the dead, no right-minded person would have glorified anything so hideous and repulsive as a cross stained with the blood of Jesus. By the miracle of His rising from the grave, Jesus placed the seal of assurance upon the forgiveness of our sins. A dead Christ could not have been our Savior. An unopened grave would never have opened heaven. By bursting the chains of the tomb, Jesus proved Himself to all ages the conqueror of sin. The sacrifice on Calvary had fulfilled its purpose; the ransom price paid for your sins and mine had been accepted by God. Hallelujah, what a Savior!

Prayer For The Day:

Each time I see the empty cross, let me
be reminded of Your suffering and Your victory, Lord Jesus.

·APRIL 6·

"Search the Book of the Lord . . ."

Isaiah 34:16 (TLB)

A knowledge of the Bible is essential to a rich and meaningful life. For the words of this Book have a way of filling in the missing pieces, of bridging the gaps, of turning the tarnished colors of our life to jewel-like brilliance. Learn to take your every problem to the Bible. Within its pages you will find the correct answer. But most of all, the Bible is a revelation of the nature of God. The philosophers of the centuries have struggled with the problem of a Supreme Being. Who is He? What is He? Where is He? If there is such a Person, is He interested in me? If so, how can I know Him? These and a thousand other questions about God are answered in this Holy Book we call the Bible.

Prayer For The Day:

> *How glorious it is to read Your Word*
> *and learn more of You, my Savior and my Lord!*

•APRIL 7•

> *"He is not here, but is risen."*
>
> Luke 24:6

Something distinguishes Christianity from all the religions of the world. Not only does it carry the truth of the redemption, by the death of our Savior for our sins on the cross, but it carries the fact that Christ rose again. Only the Christian faith claims that its Leader died and rose again and is alive at this moment. Many gravestones carry the inscription, "Here lies . . .," but on Christ's tomb are emblazoned the words, "He is not here." Christianity has no shrines to visit, no dusty remains to venerate, no tombs at which to worship. Many good men have lived, and still live, in the memory of those who knew them, but there is only one Man who conquered death—Jesus Christ—and He will live forever.

Prayer For The Day:

> *The account of Your resurrection*
> *never ceases to bring me joy, Lord Jesus.*

•APRIL 8•

> *"Look! There is the Lamb of God*
> *who takes away the world's sin."*
>
> John 1:29 (TLB)

At the cross of Christ, sin reached its climax. Its most terrible display took place at Calvary. It was never blacker or more hideous. We see the human heart laid bare and its corruption fully exposed. Some people have said that man has improved since that day, that if Christ came back today, He would not be crucified but would be given a glorious reception. Christ does come to us every day in the form of Bibles that we do not read, in the form of churches that we do not attend, in the form of human need that we pass by. I am convinced that if Christ came back today, He would be crucified more quickly than He was two thousand years ago. Sin never improves. Human nature has not changed.

Prayer For The Day:

Father, take away my thoughts
and deeds that crucify Jesus afresh.

•APRIL 9•

"And when they were come
to the place which is called Calvary,
there they crucified him . . ."

Luke 23:33

O ne of the ironies of human nature is that it often has a way of rejecting the best and accepting the worst. Why did the crowd ask for the release of Barabbas and the crucifixion of Jesus? The answer is in the biblical statement, "The heart is deceitful above all things, and desperately wicked." Jesus is just as divine today and just as much alive as He was on that first Good Friday. Yet millions today don't accept Him. His goodness is still a rebuke to our badness; His purity still shows up our impurities; His sinlessness still reveals our sinfulness; and unless we allow Him to destroy the evil within us, the evil within us still wants to destroy Him. This is the conflict of the ages.

Prayer For The Day:

Lord Jesus, when I reflect upon
the agony of Your death at Calvary, my heart
is once again humbled at the magnitude of Your love
for all mankind.

•APRIL 10•

"For if there is no resurrection of the dead,
then Christ must still be dead. And if he is still
dead, then all our preaching is useless and your
trust in God is empty, worthless, hopeless. . . .
The fact is that Christ did actually rise from the dead
. . ."

1 Corinthians 15:13,14,20 (TLB)

I was invited to have coffee one morning with Konrad Adenauer before he retired as the Chancellor of Germany. When I walked in, I expected to meet a tall, stiff, formal man who might even be embarrassed if I brought up the subject of religion. After the greeting, the Chancellor suddenly turned to me and said, "Mr. Graham, what is the most important thing in the world?" Before I could answer, he had answered his own question. He said, "The resurrection of Jesus Christ. If Jesus Christ is alive, then there is hope for the world. If Jesus Christ is in the grave, then I don't see the slightest glimmer of hope on the horizon." Then he amazed me by saying that he believed that the resurrection of Christ was one of the best-attested facts of history. He said, "When I leave office, I intend to spend the rest of my life gathering scientific proof of the resurrection of Jesus Christ." It was the fact of the resurrection of Christ that called the disciples to go out as burning young revolutionaries to change the world of their day. They preached that Christ is alive. This should be our message, not only on Easter, but on every day of the year.

Prayer For The Day:

Father, let my message to others be that
of the resurrection of the Lord Jesus Christ and
of His ability to change the lives of those who believe in Him.

•APRIL 11•

"He hath made him to be
sin for us . . . that we might be made
the righteousness of God . . ."
        2 Corinthians 5:21

Augustine was one of the greatest theologians of all time. He was a wild, intemperate, immoral youth. In spite of his mother's pleadings and prayers, he grew worse instead of better. But one day he had a personal encounter with Jesus Christ that transformed his life. His restlessness and the practice of sin disappeared. He became one of the great saints of all time. John Newton was a slave trader on the west coast of Africa. One day in a storm at sea he met Jesus Christ. He went back to England and became an Anglican clergyman. He wrote scores of hymns, one of which has become the modern popular song, "Amazing Grace." This is what Christ can do for anyone who puts his trust in Him.

Prayer For The Day:

Your amazing grace transformed
even my unworthy life—I love You, Lord Jesus!

·APRIL 12·

*"Let your light so shine before men,
that they may see your good works, and
glorify your Father which is in heaven."*

Matthew 5:16

One faithful witness is worth a thousand mute professors of religion. Tom Allan, Scotland's famous young preacher, was brought to Christ while a black soldier was singing, "Were You There When They Crucified My Lord?" He said it was neither the song nor the voice, but the spirit in which that soldier sang—something about his manner, something about his sincerity of expression—that convicted him of his wicked life and turned him to the Savior. Our faith grows by expression. If we want to keep our faith, we must share it—we must witness.

Prayer For The Day:

*May others be drawn to You,
Lord Jesus, as I tell them of Your love.*

·APRIL 13·

*"Brethren . . . present your
bodies a living sacrifice, holy, acceptable unto
God, which is your reasonable service."*

Romans 12:1

In a book called *The Age of Longing* we read that an American girl married a radical revolutionary in Paris. She had lost her faith at an American University—lost all the religious faith she had, and all the things her parents had told her. She was asked why she married him. She said, "He's the first person I have ever known who believes something strong enough to die for it. Although I don't believe exactly as he does, I was attracted to this man who had found a cause." I find that young people today are looking for a cause, and they are not looking for something easy. Some time ago a university student in Moscow told one of my colleagues, "You Christians say that you are going to win the world, but we've done more in fifty years than you've done in two thousand years. And do you know why? It is because you are not committed. We are. We will win, you'll see."

Prayer For The Day:

*I look at my dedication to You, Jesus,
my Lord and Savior, and am ashamed—You gave
everything for me. May I always live totally committed
in love to You.*

•APRIL 14•

*"Our homeland is in heaven,
where our Savior the Lord Jesus Christ is; and
we are looking forward to his return . . ."*
      Philippians 3:20 (TLB)

The Scriptures indicate that we are living in man's day. But there is coming a day that will be called the Day of the Lord. In the midst of hopelessness, there is hope! And that hope is centered in the God-man, the Lord Jesus Christ. Now the will of man runs riot in the earth. Then the will of the Lord will alone be done. Until that time, we are under orders from the King of kings to proclaim His message. When we engage in evangelism, we are obeying His great command to "go and proclaim " In doing so, we are hastening the day of His return.

Prayer For The Day:

*As I live in the hope of Your return,
give me the wisdom and love to reach those around me.*

•APRIL 15•

*"I am he that liveth, and was dead;
and, behold, I am alive for evermore . . ."*
      Revelation 1:18

Certain laws of evidence hold in the establishment of any historic event. Documentation of the event in question must be made by reliable contemporary witnesses. There is more evidence that Jesus rose from the dead than there is that Julius Caesar ever lived, or that Alexander the Great died at the age of 33. It is strange that historians will accept thousands of facts for which they can produce only shreds of evidence. But in the face of the overwhelming evidence of the resurrection of Jesus Christ, they cast a skeptical eye and hold intellectual doubts. The trouble with many people is that they do not *want* to believe. They are so completely prejudiced that they cannot accept the glorious fact of the resurrection of Christ on Bible testimony alone.

Prayer For The Day:

> *Lord Jesus, I know You are alive—*
> *for You live in the hearts of all those who love You!*

• APRIL 16 •

> *"Behold, I am with thee, and will*
> *keep thee in all places whither thou goest."*
> *Genesis 28:15*

When Jesus uttered His words of comfort in the first few verses of the fourteenth chapter of John's Gospel, concluding with, "And whither I go ye know, and the way ye know" (John 14:4), Thomas said unto Him, "Lord, we know not whither thou goest; and how can we know the way?" (John 14:5). Jesus answered him with a statement which has in it the ring of eternity. It was sublimely simple and yet profoundly deep. Its surface meaning was clear to all, and yet the great theologians have never completely sounded its mighty depths. This is that statement, "I am the way, the truth, and the life; no man cometh unto the Father, but by me" (John 14:6). In one majestic sweep, these words silenced Thomas' questioning tongue and brought reassurance and peace to the hearts of the other disciples. Within the marvel of that authoritative sentence from the lips of the Son of God, there was enough comfort to assuage the sufferings of the tormented, enough wisdom to satisfy those who yearned for understanding, and enough power to set the great Christian movement in motion.

Prayer For The Day:

> *Knowing You are with me is all the comfort I need, Lord.*

· APRIL 17 ·

*"He which raised up the
Lord Jesus shall raise up us also by Jesus . . ."*
2 Corinthians 4:14

The resurrection of Christ brings hope. The late Emil Brunner once said, "What oxygen is for the lungs, such is hope for the meaning of human life." As the human organism is dependent on a supply of oxygen, so humanity is dependent on its supply of hope. Yet today hopelessness and despair are everywhere. Peter, who himself was given to despair during the episode of Calvary, writes in a triumphant note, "Blessed be the God and Father of our Lord Jesus Christ, who according to His abundant mercy hath begotten us again into a lively hope by the resurrection of Jesus Christ from the dead." There is hope that mistakes and sins can be forgiven. There is hope that we can have joy, peace, assurance, and security in the midst of the despair of this age. There is hope that Christ is coming soon—this is what is called in Scripture "the blessed hope." There is hope that there will come some day a new heaven and a new earth, and that the Kingdom of God will reign and triumph. Our hope is not in our own ability, or in our goodness, or in our physical strength. Our hope is instilled in us by the resurrection of Christ.

Prayer For The Day:

*My hope is in You, my resurrected Lord and Savior,
Jesus Christ! May I never despair, as I remember
Your triumph and love.*

· APRIL 18 ·

*". . . realize that your
heavenly Father will . . . give the Holy Spirit
to those who ask for him."*
Luke 11:13 (TLB)

Before He left His disciples, Christ promised that He would send a Comforter to help them in the trials, cares, and temptations of life. This word comforter means "one that helps alongside." He is the Holy Spirit, the powerful Third Person of the Trinity. The moment you are born again, He takes up residence in your heart. You may not emotionally feel Him there, but you must exercise faith. Believe it! Accept it as a fact of faith! He is in your heart to help you. We are told that He sheds the love of God abroad in our hearts. He produces the fruit of the Spirit: "love, joy, peace, long-suffering, gentleness, goodness, faith, meekness, temperance." We cannot possibly manufacture this fruit in our own strength. It is supernaturally manufactured by the Holy Spirit who lives in our hearts!

Prayer For The Day:

Lord God Almighty, I praise You for
Your Holy Spirit who guides and keeps me in all my ways.

⋆APRIL 19⋆

"I advise you to obey only the Holy Spirit's
instructions. He will tell you where to go and
what to do, and then you won't always be doing
the wrong things your evil nature wants you to."
Galatians 5:16 (TLB)

To walk in the Spirit is a challenging and inspiring exercise, for it combines activity with relaxation. To walk means to place one foot in front of the other. If you stop doing this, you are no longer walking—you are standing still. Walking always implies movement, progress, and direction. Sin shall no longer rule or dominate you when you are allowing the Holy Spirit to live Christ's life through you. It is living by faith, living by trust, living in dependence upon God. If we look to our own resources, our own strength or our own ability, as Peter did when he walked on the water, we will fail. You cannot live the Christian life by yourself. The Holy Spirit must live in you and express Himself through you. Living for Christ is a day-by-day experience. It is a continuous dependence upon the Spirit of God. It is believing in His faithfulness.

Prayer For The Day:

Lord, so often I have walked
on my own instead of walking in
Your Spirit. Guide my footsteps this day, I pray in Jesus' name.

• APRIL 20 •

". . . he hath set his love upon me . . ."
                              Psalm 91:14

A basic need of mankind is affection. Those who "abide in Him" are objects of God's affection and love. You cannot say that you are friendless when Christ has said, "Henceforth I call you not servants . . . but I have called you friends" (John 15:15). To you who lament the fact that you have been bereft of affection and love in this life, I happily commend Christ. He loved you enough to lay down His life for you. Not only that, but by His atonement upon the cross, He purchased the favor of God in your behalf, and now through Him you may be the recipient of the grace and love of God without measure.

Prayer For The Day:

Thank You for Your love,
Father, that no matter where I am—
in whatever situation—You are there, loving me.

• APRIL 21 •

"Be full of love for others,
following the example of Christ . . ."
                              Ephesians 5:2 (TLB)

There is no doubt that we need social reform. If success is ever to be realized, our generations must work together and listen to each other, which is one of the first requirements of cooperation. At this point, the Gospel of Jesus Christ is relevant as the great reconciler. The Apostle John, in his first epistle, declared, "To you, young men, I have written," and, "To you, fathers, I have written." This is to the young activists and to the old guard, "It is by this that we know what love is: that Christ laid down His life for us. And we in our turn are bound to lay down our lives for our brothers. But if a man has enough to live on, and yet when he sees his brother in need shuts up his heart against him, how can it be said that the divine love dwells in him? My children, love must not be a matter of words or talk; it must be genuine, and show itself in action. This is how we may know that we belong to the realm of truth" (1 John 3:16-19, NEB).

Prayer For The Day:

Father, when someone disagrees with
my opinions, may my love not be determined by
rhetoric, but by the all-encompassing love
of Your Son, Jesus Christ.

*Dallis died
today in 2001*

• APRIL 22 •

"Don't worry about anything; instead
pray about everything; tell God your needs
and don't forget to thank him for his answers."
Philippians 4:6 (TLB)

Historians will probably call our era "the age of anxiety." Anxiety is the natural result when our hopes are centered in anything short of God and His will for us. When we make anything else our goal, frustration and defeat are inevitable. Though we have less to worry about than previous generations, we have more worry. Though we have it easier than our forefathers, we have more uneasiness. Though we have less real cause for anxiety than our predecessors, we are inwardly more anxious. Calloused hands were the badge of the pioneer, but a furrowed brow is the insignia of modern man. God has never promised to remove all our troubles, problems, and difficulties. In fact, sometimes I think the truly committed Christian is in conflict with the society around him more than any other person. Society is going in one direction, and the Christian is going in the opposite direction. This brings about friction and conflict. But God has promised, in the midst of trouble and conflict, a genuine peace, a sense of assurance and security, that the worldly person never knows.

Prayer For The Day:

Lord Jesus, teach me to keep my eyes
centered on You rather than on myself and my anxieties.
Help me to allow You to give me peace of heart and mind today.

• APRIL 23 •

"I, even I, am he that comforteth you . . ."
                                    Isaiah 51:12

There is also comfort in mourning, because in the midst of mourning God gives a song. His presence in our lives changes our mourning into song, and that song is a song of comfort. This kind of comfort is the kind which enabled a devout Englishman to look at a deep dark hole in the ground where his home stood before the bombing and say, "I always did want a basement. Now I can jolly well build another house, like I always wanted." This kind of comfort is the kind which enabled a young minister's wife in a church near us to teach her Sunday school class of girls on the very day of her husband's funeral. Her mourning was not the kind which had no hope—it was a mourning of faith in the goodness and wisdom of God; it believed that our heavenly Father makes no mistakes.

Prayer For The Day:

Oh heavenly Father, who knows what
agony and grief are because of
the sacrifice of Your beloved Son, Jesus Christ—
I thank You for the comfort which embraces all those
who love You.

• APRIL 24 •

". . . when they found him not,
they turned back again to Jerusalem . . ."
                                    Luke 2:45

We might as well face it, strife has even infiltrated our church life. It is true enough that the Church is now the Church militant. But, as such, its warfare ought to be that of dedication to revealed truth and divine holiness, and not intramural bickering and carnal disputes. We read in the second chapter of Luke that Joseph and Mary lost Jesus one day. Where did they lose Him? They lost Him in the most unlikely place in all the world—the Temple. I have seen many people lose Jesus right in the church. I have seen them lose Him in a dispute about who was to be choir director, who was to play the organ, who was to be an elder, or who was to be the minister. Yes, because we are human, though Christian, it is easy to lose sight of Jesus right in the temple!

Prayer For The Day:

> *Don't let me lose sight of You, Lord,*
> *in the complex logistics of everyday life.*

✦APRIL 25✦

> *"We . . . offer our sacrifice of praise to God*
> *by telling others of the glory of his name."*
> *Hebrews 13:15 (TLB)*

J esus knew that one of the real tests of our yieldedness to God is our willingness to share with others. If we have no mercy toward others, that is one proof that we have never experienced God's mercy. Emerson must have been reading the gauge of human mercy when he said, "What you are speaks so loud that I cannot hear what you say." Satan does not care how much you theorize about Christianity, or how much you profess to know Christ. What he opposes vigorously is the way you *live* Christ. Some time ago a lady wrote and said, "I am 65 years old. My children are all married, my husband is dead, and I am one of the loneliest people in all the world." It was suggested to her that she find a way of sharing her religious faith and her material goods with those around her. She wrote a few weeks later and said, "I am the happiest woman in town. I have found a new joy and happiness in sharing with others." That's exactly what Jesus promised!

Prayer For The Day:

> *There is no greater joy, Father,*
> *than sharing Your love. Help me*
> *to convey this in all my dealings with others.*

·APRIL 26·

"The heavens declare the glory of God;
and the firmament sheweth his handiwork.
Day unto day uttereth speech, and night unto
night sheweth knowledge. There is no speech
nor language, where their voice is not heard."
Psalm 19:1-3

There is a language in nature that speaks of the existence of God. It is the language of order, beauty, perfection, and intelligence. Some time ago a scientist told me that when he gave serious thought to the majestic order of the universe and its obedience to unchanging law, he could not help but believe in God. He had become aware that God was speaking through nature. God speaks in the certainty and regularity of the seasons; in the precision of the movements of the sun, the moon, and the stars; in the regular coming of night and day; in the balance between man's consumption of life-giving oxygen and its production by the plant life of the earth; and even in the cry of a newborn child with its ever-new dimension of the miracle of life.

Prayer For The Day:

The beauty of this day will
be a constant reminder of the magnificence of You, God.

·APRIL 27·

"I am like a sheltered olive tree
protected by the Lord himself. I trust in the
mercy of God forever and ever."
Psalm 52:8 (TLB)

Turn to your Bible and read the wonderful stories of men who were alone in godless surroundings but who, by the help and presence of the living God, made a marvelous contribution to their own times. Joseph was surrounded by sin and intrigue in Egypt. His master's wife tried to seduce him. He was tested by imprisonment, but through it all he trusted in God and sought to know and do His will; and he stands today as a wonderful example of the keeping and strengthening power of God in the heart of a man who believed in Him.

Prayer For The Day:

In the dark days, I will put out
my hand and You, loving Lord, will be there.

• APRIL 28 •

"Who gave himself for our sins . . ."
Galatians 1:4

Years ago King Charles V was loaned a large sum of money by a merchant in Antwerp. The note came due, but the King was bankrupt and unable to pay. The merchant gave a great banquet for the King. When all the guests were seated and before the food was brought in, the merchant had a large platter placed on the table and a fire lighted on it. Then, taking the note out of his pocket, he held it in the flames until it was burned to ashes. The king threw his arms around his benefactor and wept. Just so, we have been mortgaged to God. The debt was due, but we were unable to pay. Two thousand years ago God invited the world to the Gospel feast, and in the agonies of the cross, God held your sins and mine until every last vestige of our guilt was consumed.

Prayer For The Day:

In gratitude I kneel before You, Lord Jesus Christ.

• APRIL 29 •

"Restore to me again the joy of your
salvation, and make me willing to obey you."
Psalm 51:12 (TLB)

It is not unusual for persons in their early twenties to defect from their early teaching. The reasons are many. Perhaps their exposure to unbelief "took" better than their exposure to belief. This is often the case, for the Bible says, "The heart of man is deceitful above all things." The human heart is as prepared by sin to accept unbelief as faith. Some person they regard highly has undoubtedly influenced their thinking; and for the time being they look on their early training as "bunk." As someone has said, "A little learning may take a man away from God, but full understanding will bring him back." Some of the staunchest Christians I know are people who had periods in their life when they questioned the Bible,

Christ, and God. But as they continued to examine the matter, there was overwhelming evidence that only "the fool hath said in his heart, There is no God."

Prayer For The Day:

> *I pray for all the questioning people today,*
> *Lord, remembering times in my own life when unbelief reigned.*

•APRIL 30•

> *"Be sober, be vigilant; because your*
> *adversary the devil, as a roaring lion, walketh*
> *about, seeking whom he may devour."*
> *1 Peter 5:8*

When I was in the hospital in Hawaii, I read again of the shocking events which led up to the destruction of the United States fleet at Pearl Harbor. On that fateful day of December 7, 1941, the Japanese attacked. We know now that that attack was invited by our failure to be always vigilant. The result was the destruction of our fleet—the cause was tragic indifference. When comfort and ease and pleasure are put ahead of duty and conviction, progress is always set back. What makes us Christians shrug our shoulders when we ought to be flexing our muscles? What makes us apathetic in a day when there are loads to lift, a world to be won, and captives to be set free? Why are so many bored, when the times demand action? Christ told us that in the last days there would be an insipid attitude toward life.

Prayer For The Day:

> *Take away the apathy,*
> *Father, that so often blinds my vision.*

•MAY 1•

> *"He will keep in perfect peace*
> *all those who trust in him, whose*
> *thoughts turn often to the Lord!"*
> *Isaiah 26:3 (TLB)*

You have an ego—a consciousness of being an individual. Of course, you do. But that doesn't mean that you are to worship yourself, to think constantly of yourself, and to live entirely for yourself. Common sense tells you that your life would be miserable if you followed that course. God is infinitely more concerned about your happiness than you could possibly be. He says, "Deny yourself, and follow me." There is many a person in the insane asylum today who thought excessively about himself, to the exclusion of God and others. Hypochondriacs who have a fanciful anxiety about their health will never be well, regardless of their physical condition.

Prayer For The Day:

*Keep my mind on You, Lord, and help me
to discipline the thoughts of self which crowd out Your peace.*

·MAY 2·

"When I consider thy heavens . . ."

Psalm 8:3

To look into a microscope is to see another universe so small that only the electronic microscope can even find it. For instance, it is revealed that one single snowflake in a snowstorm with millions of other snowflakes is the equivalent of twenty billion electrons. Scientists are learning that the miniature world of a single living cell is as astonishing as man himself. God says that we can learn a great deal about Him just by observing nature. Because He has spoken through His universe, all men are without excuse for not believing in Him. This is why the Psalmist said, "The fool hath said in his heart, There is no God" (Psalm 14:1).

Prayer For The Day:

*The infinitesimal beauty of
Your creation speaks to my heart of the
certainty of Your presence, almighty and everlasting God.*

•MAY 3•

"Only a fool would say to himself, 'There
is no God.' And why does he say it? Because of
his wicked heart, his dark and evil deeds.
His life is corroded with sin."

Psalm 53:1 (TLB)

We live like a little ant on this little speck of dust out in space. We get a Ph.D. degree and we strut across the stage and say, "Well, I don't know whether or not there is a God." And we can't even control ourselves. We can't even keep from blowing ourselves apart. We can't even keep from manufacturing nuclear weapons that could destroy the world. We can't even keep from hating each other, and fighting with each other, and killing each other. We can't even keep from stealing from each other. We can't even keep from dying, because all of us are going to die. No wonder the Bible says, "The fool hath said in his heart, There is no God," because a man that would deny the existence of God is a fool.

Prayer For The Day:

Almighty God, help me to live in
such a way, that when I tell others of Your existence,
they will be drawn to acknowledge and receive You.

•MAY 4•

"But now in Christ Jesus ye who
sometimes were far off are made nigh by the
blood of Christ. For he is our peace . . ."

Ephesians 2:13,14

Meaningless mouthings about peace will not bring it to the world. In Glasgow, Scotland, we watched the Communists march around St. George's Square carrying their banners with the words, "Our motto is PEACE!" My thoughts raced back to Korea, where I had seen the havoc and suffering caused by these people who now use "peace" as their motto. Peace is more than five little white letters painted on a piece of red cloth, carried by a goose-stepping zealot in a Red parade. It is not a mere cessation of hostilities, a momentary halt in a hot or cold war. Rather, it is something positive. It is a specific relationship with God into which a person is brought. It is a spiritual reality in a human heart which has come into vital contact with the infinite God.

Prayer For The Day:

Your everlasting peace
transcends the promises of mankind, Lord Jesus.

⋆MAY 5⋆

"Keep yourselves in the love of God . . ."
Jude 21

A husband and wife visited an orphanage where they hoped to adopt a child. In an interview with the boy they wanted, they told him in glowing terms about the many things they could give him. To their amazement the little fellow said, "If you have nothing to offer except a good home, clothes, toys, and the other things that most kids have—why, I would just as soon stay here." "What on earth could you want besides those things?" the woman asked. "I just want someone to love me," replied the little boy. There you have it! Even a little boy knows that "man shall not live by bread alone." Our deeper yearnings and longings can be met only by a renewed fellowship with the One in whose image we were created, God.

Prayer For The Day:

Thank You for loving me, God.
This knowledge never ceases to amaze me.
I praise and love You, my heavenly Father.

⋆MAY 6⋆

"Know ye that the Lord, he is
God; it is he that hath made us and
not we ourselves . . ."
Psalm 100:3

W henever anyone asks me how I can be so certain about who and what God really is, I am reminded of the story of the little boy who was out flying a kite. It was a fine day to go kite-flying, the wind was brisk, and large billowy clouds were blowing across the sky. The kite went up and up until it was entirely hidden by the clouds. "What are you doing?" a man asked the little boy. "I'm flying a kite," he replied. "Flying a kite, are you?" the man said, "How can you be sure? You can't see your kite." "No," said the little boy, "I can't see it, but every little while I feel a tug, so I know for sure that it's there!" Don't take anyone else's word for God. Find Him for yourself, and then you too will know by the wonderful, warm tug on your heartstring, that He is there, for sure.

Prayer For The Day:

Oh heavenly Father,
as I reach out to You I feel
the "tug" of Your Holy Spirit, which tells me of Your presence!

·MAY 7·

"If the Son therefore shall
make you free, ye shall be free indeed."
John 8:36

The mark of a true Christian is found in his personal relationship to the Person of Jesus Christ. Christianity is Christ. Christ is Christianity. I speak reverently when I say that Jesus is more than His ideas. All that He said was true, but without Him even the truth would have been powerless. Men know the power of truth, and truth is that which sets men free. Jesus said, "I am the truth."

Prayer For The Day:

Thank You, Jesus, for the
shackles that have been broken in my life!

·MAY 8·

"Her children arise
up, and call her blessed . . ."
Proverbs 31:28

Only God Himself fully appreciates the influence of a Christian mother in the molding of character in her children. Someone has said, "Like mother, like children." Most of the noble characters and fine leaders of history have had good, God-fearing mothers. We are told that George Washington's mother was pious, and that Sir Walter Scott's mother was a lover of poetry and music. On the other hand, we are told that Nero's mother was a murderess and that the dissolute Lord Byron's mother was a proud and violent woman. The influence of a mother upon the lives of her children cannot be measured. They know and absorb her example and attitudes when it comes to questions of honesty, temperance, kindness, and industry.

Prayer For The Day:

Thank You, Lord, for mothers
who love You. Their influence is felt around the world.

◆MAY 9◆

"The kingdoms of this world are become
the kingdoms of our Lord, and of his Christ;
and he shall reign for ever and ever."
Revelation 11:15

C hristianity is a Gospel of crisis. It proclaims unmistakably that this world's days are numbered. Every graveyard and every cemetery testify that the Bible is true. Our days on this planet are numbered. The Apostle James says that life is only a vapor that appears for a moment and then vanishes (James 4:14). The prophet Isaiah says that our life is like the grass that withers and the flower that fades (Isaiah 40:6,7). There is no doubt that nations also come to an end when they have ceased to fulfill the function that God meant for them. The end will come with the return of Jesus Christ. He will set up a kingdom of righteousness and social justice where hatred, greed, jealousy, and death will no longer be known. That is why a Christian can be an optimist. That is why a Christian can smile in the midst of all that is happening. We know what will come. We know what the end will be: the triumph of the Lord Jesus Christ!

Prayer For The Day:

While the world around me is in such turmoil,
Your peace lives in my heart, as I look for Your triumphant return!

·MAY 10·

"Everything comes from God alone.
Everything lives by his power, and everything is
for his glory. To him be glory evermore."
Romans 11:36 (TLB)

Have you ever wondered why God placed us on this planet? What our purpose is in being here? It is because God is love. There may be life on other planets, but I believe man is unique in the sense that he was created in the image of God. God created on this planet as it were "little gods" whom He could love and who would return love to Him. Reverently speaking, God was lonely. He wanted someone to love and who would return love to Him. That sounds incredible, but the Bible tells us that God loved, and so He created and put us on this planet.

Prayer For The Day:

> *Freely I love You, divine God,*
> *who daily brings joy to my soul.*

·MAY 11·

"Heaven and earth shall pass away,
but my words shall not pass away."
Matthew 24:35

Time is running out. The seconds are ticking away toward midnight. The human race is about to take the fatal plunge. Which way shall we turn? Is there any authority left? Is there a path we can follow? Can we find a code book that will give us the key to our dilemmas? Is there any source of authority to which we can turn? Have we just been placed here by some unknown creator or force without any clue as to where we came from, why we are here, and where we are going? The answer is "no." We do have a code book. We do have a key. We do have authoritative source material. It is found in the ancient and historic Book we call the Bible. This Book has come down to us through the ages. It has passed through so many hands, appeared in so many forms—and survived attack of every kind. Neither barbaric vandalism nor civilized scholarship has touched it. Neither the burning of fire nor the laughter of skepticism has accomplished its annihilation. Through the many dark ages of man its glorious promises have survived unchanged.

Prayer For The Day:

*How often I take for granted the privilege
of being able to read my Bible. Forgive me, Lord.*

·MAY 12·

*". . . that I may open my mouth boldly,
to make known the mystery of the gospel."*

Ephesians 6:19

The word "mystery" means beyond human knowledge or understanding. God's mysteries baffle the unbelieving, but bless the believer. The mystery of righteousness, like some of the other great mysteries of God, we cannot comprehend, but we know it works. We stand amazed at this great mystery which enables God to change the human heart, its attitudes, its desires, and its nature. God, a holy God, who loves righteousness and hates wickedness, through a process of redemption has refashioned us in the image of Himself. How marvelous! For generations He has been applying His righteousness to the hearts of men. Even in our time, with its complexities of living, God is in the business of changing men and women by the mystery of righteousness.

Prayer For The Day:

*Give me Your boldness to tell
others the secret of eternal joy in Jesus Christ.*

·MAY 13·

*"Ye call me Master and Lord:
and ye say well; for so I am."*

John 13:13

He (the Spirit) will never lead you contrary to the Word of God. I hear people saying, "The Lord led me to do this. . . . The Lord told me thus and so . . ." I am always a little suspicious unless what the Lord has said is in keeping with His Word. God never directs us to do anything contrary to His Word. The prophet Samuel once said, "Obedience is better than sacrifice." The Scripture teaches, "He that willeth to do His will shall know the doctrine." When you find yourself up a blind alley, not knowing which way to turn, if you are willing to do His will, He will reveal Himself. He conceals His will only from those who, before they consent to do His bidding, seek to know what He is going to say. Be an obedient Christian. Remember that "where God guides, He provides. Where He leads, He supplies all needs!"

Prayer For The Day:

Let me be acutely attuned to Your Word, so that each decision I have to make will be in Your will, almighty God.

•MAY 14•

"Be kindly affectioned one to another with brotherly love . . ."
Romans 12:10

Living creatively for Christ in the home is the acid test for any Christian man or woman. It is far easier to live an excellent life among your friends, when you are putting your best foot forward and are conscious of public opinion, than it is to live for Christ in your home. Your own family circle knows whether Christ lives in you and through you. If you are a true Christian, you will not give way at home to bad temper, impatience, fault-finding, sarcasm, unkindness, suspicion, selfishness, or laziness. Instead, you will reveal through your daily life the fruit of the Spirit, which is love, joy, peace, long-suffering, and all the other Christian virtues which round out a Christlike personality.

Prayer For The Day:

My family, Lord, knows the real me— they deserve so much more. May I live so close to You that Your love will flow through me to them.

•MAY 15•

*"... all our righteousnesses
are as filthy rags ..."*

Isaiah 64:6

The Bible teaches that all our righteousness—falling short of the divine standard as it does—is as filthy rags in the sight of God. There is absolutely no possibility of our manufacturing a righteousness, holiness, or goodness that will satisfy God. Even the best of us is impure to God. I remember one day when my wife was doing the washing. The clothes looked white and clean in the house, but when she hung them on the line they appeared soiled and dirty, in contrast to the fresh-fallen snow. Our own lives may seem at times to be morally good and decent; but in comparison to the holiness and the purity of God, we are defiled and filthy. In spite of our sins and moral uncleanness God loves us. He decided to provide a righteousness for us. That is the reason that He gave His Son, Jesus Christ, to die on the cross.

Prayer For The Day:

*My life is like a gray pall beside
the whiteness of Your purity, Lord Jesus. Cleanse me this day.*

•MAY 16•

*"Wherefore the law was our
schoolmaster to bring us unto Christ, that
we might be justified by faith."*

Galatians 3:24

When God gave the law, He knew that man was incapable of keeping it. Many persons are confused as to why God gave the law, if He knew man could not possibly keep it. The Bible teaches that the law was given as a mirror; I look into the law and see my spiritual condition. I see how far short I come, and this drives me to the cross of Christ for forgiveness. The Bible teaches that this is why Christ came—to redeem them that were under the law. Man could not keep the law, he was condemned by the law.

Prayer For The Day:

*How I need Your guidelines, Lord.
Teach me to be always mindful of Your leading.*

·MAY 17·

". . . doing service as to the Lord . . ."

Ephesians 6:7

A true sacrament is not a mere creed, or ordinance, or form, but it is a life of service to God and to man. The most eloquent prayer is the prayer through hands that heal and bless. The highest form of worship is the worship of unselfish Christian service. The greatest form of praise is the sound of consecrated feet seeking out the lost and helpless. There must be a practical outworking of our faith here in this present world, or it will never endure the world to come. The Pharisees majored on show but minored on service. We need fewer words and more charitable works; less palaver and more pity; less repetition of creed and more compassion.

Prayer For The Day:

Talk so often drowns out the cries for help—
I am guilty of this, Lord. I would worship You in
everything I do. Extend my hands with Your mercy, Lord.

·MAY 18·

". . . let us stop just
saying we love people; let us really love
them, and show it by our actions."

1 John 3:18 (TLB)

The Bible declares that we who follow Christ should be just as much in love with each other as God was in love with us when He sent His Son to die on the cross. The moment we come to Christ, Scripture says, God gives us supernatural love that is shed abroad in our hearts by the Holy Spirit. The greatest demonstration of the fact that we are Christians is that we love one another. Why not go out of our way to be a friend to someone whose skin is a different color from ours? Love does more to solve our problems than anything else does. Of all the gifts God offers His children, love is the greatest. Of all the fruits of the Holy Spirit, love is the first.

Prayer For The Day:

Jesus, loving Lord, teach me real love—
mine is often shallow in my relationship to others.

·MAY 19·

". . . serving the Lord; rejoicing in hope . . ."
Romans 12:11,12

Each generation becomes more addicted to the sedatives of life, to dull the pain of living. Oppressed by a sense of triviality and thwarted purpose, men find no great goal or commitment to draw them, and no inner stimulation to give meaning to their existence. Christ can save you from the bane of boredom. He waits to give you a fresh sense of direction and to take dissatisfaction out of your life. I talked recently with a man in my own community who was converted to faith in Christ. "I hadn't known what to do with my leisure time," he told me, "but now I have a sense of commitment and purpose that I never knew before."

Prayer For The Day:

Even the smallest job I do today is part
of my service to You, Lord. Help my heart to be so
filled with Your Spirit I will rejoice whatever task is set before me.

·MAY 20·

". . . greater is he that
is in you, than he that is in the world."
1 John 4:4

Paul once wrote, "For the flesh lusteth against the Spirit and the Spirit against the flesh; and these are contrary the one to the other; so that ye can not do the things that ye would" (Galatians 5:17). This is the battle or the tension that is present in us to a greater or lesser degree. So, you see, the spiritual lag that you feel is explained in the Bible. That does not mean that you accept it as the way it should be. You should make all necessary preparations for this battle which the Bible says "is not against flesh and blood, but against spiritual forces." In Ephesians 6 we read that the Bible tells what preparation you should make. In the meantime, always remember that "where sin abounds, grace did much more abound." You can have complete victory! We are told to submit ourselves unto God, and the devil will flee from us. We are also promised that "sin shall not reign over us."

Prayer For The Day:

Lord, like Paul I battle
daily with Satan. I submit everything in
my life to You, knowing that already the fight has been won.

•MAY 21•

"Come to Christ, who is the living
Foundation of Rock upon which God builds;
though men have spurned him, he is very
precious to God who has chosen him above all
others."
                                                    1 Peter 2:4 (TLB)

No personality in history stands above Jesus Christ. Agnostics and atheists have found fault with Christian ideas, but they can never find fault with the Person of Jesus Christ. They have found fault with Christians, but not with Christ. Jesus of Nazareth transcends methods, ideas, and followers. He stands at the turning point of time. Men everywhere must bow to His superiority. Since Christianity is Christ, those who wish to be a Christian must accept and follow Him as a Person. He and He alone is able to meet every need of the human race.

Prayer For The Day:

Only You, Lord Jesus, meet all
the needs in the hearts of men. You have met ·
mine in all the loneliest and all the happiest moments of my life.

•MAY 22•

"Our soul waiteth for the Lord . . ."
                                                    Psalm 33:20

I am a soul—and I have a body! The body is the house in which the soul lives. When Oliver Wendell Holmes was in his 80th year, a friend hailed him and asked, "How are you?" "I'm fine," said Holmes, "the house I live in is tottering and crumbling, but Oliver Wendell Holmes is fine, thank you." In this materialistic age we often forget that the real, the abiding part of us is invisible. Much time, money, and effort are expended to perpetuate the physical part of us, and too many are unconcerned about their spiritual health and nurture. Hence doctors' offices are overcrowded, and many ministers' counseling rooms are empty. When God created man, He made him distinctive, different from the other animals. "He breathed into him the breath of life and man became a living soul." He clothed him with intelligence, conscience, and a will. He made him like Himself—a companion, a friend of God. At the resurrection, this mortal shall put on immortality, and we shall be like Him, and be with Him forever.

Prayer For The Day:

What expectation is mine as
I think of being with You forever, my beloved Lord Jesus!

·MAY 23·

". . . Thou shalt love the Lord
thy God. . . . Thou shalt love thy neighbor . . ."
Matthew 22:37-39

Here is the answer to the world's problems today—"Thou shalt love the Lord thy God," "Thou shalt love thy fellowman." That teaching is not out-of-date; it is absolutely relevant today. It is the only way in which the problems of the world today can be solved, whether the problems are those of individuals or of nations. If we love God with all our heart, we will have a capacity to love our neighbors. True love will find an outlet in service—not merely in singing hymns, attending church, or even in praying— but in trying our utmost to prove our love, by obeying the will of our heavenly Father.

Prayer For The Day:

True love demands everything I have.
Take all the hidden things in my life that
keep me from loving You and my neighbor
as I should. Let me obey Your will unequivocally, dear Lord.

•MAY 24•

". . . when troubles come . . .
sing his praises with much joy."
Psalm 27:5,6 (TLB)

Christians are not altogether immune from depression. The fact is: the trend of events and the mounting tide of evil are enough to give one sobering thoughts—Christian or not. David, the sweet singer of Israel, was not always on top of his depression. Sometimes his gay, glad song was turned to a depressive mourning. "My tears have been my meat day and night, while continually they say unto me, Where is thy God? Why art thou cast down, O my soul, and why art thou disquieted in me?" I find that the cure for depression is praise. In other words: be so busy counting your blessings, that thoughts of gloom and despair will be crowded out.

Prayer For The Day:

Thank You, heavenly Father, for the
Psalms which help me see that even in the depths David
talked with You. Whatever my circumstances, I will learn to praise
You.

•May 25•

". . . to know the love of Christ,
which passeth knowledge, that ye might be
filled with all the fullness of God."
Ephesians 3:19

To appreciate art, one must either be born with an artistic sense or develop it by training. Only a relatively few people have an innate sense of color, form, and harmony. To such, a love for art comes naturally. Without an artistic appreciation in one's soul, visiting an art gallery can be a boring affair. Likewise, to appreciate good music one must have music "in him" or develop it. Without a sense of music appreciation, it is possible to sleep through a symphony concert or a performance of the Metropolitan Opera. So it is with the things of God. Talk about God can become dreary and lackluster if God isn't in you. Church can become a drab thing and the Bible an irksome Book if the Holy Spirit does not illuminate your soul with His indwelling presence. The wonderful thing about it all is that God has planned life so that if our hearts are dead to spiritual things, something can be done about it.

Prayer For The Day:

Lord God Almighty, may I daily
reach out to You and be filled with the love of Christ.

•MAY 26•

"You have your life through
Christ Jesus. He showed us God's
plan of salvation; he was the one
who made us acceptable to God . . ."
1 Corinthians 1:30 (TLB)

More and more I am becoming aware of the truth that people change people as much as ideas change people. The power of personality is strong. One could find many illustrations to prove that often personality is greater than the idea. Such is the case with Christianity. The secret of the power of Christianity is not in its ethics. It is not in Christian ideas or philosophy, although Christianity has a philosophical set of ideas. The secret of Christianity is found in a Person, and that Person is the Lord Jesus Christ. Men have discovered other philosophical and ethical systems, but they have not found another Jesus Christ. No one in history can match Him.

Prayer For The Day:

When I tell others of Your love,
help me to hide my personality in Yours, Lord Jesus.

•MAY 27•

"Follow after the
things which make for peace, and things
wherewith one may edify another."
Romans 14:19

The home is basically a sacred institution. The perfect marriage is a uniting of three persons—a man and a woman and God. That is what makes marriage holy. Faith in Christ is the most important of all principles in the building of a happy marriage and a successful home. The secret strength of a nation is found in the faith that abides in the hearts and homes of the country.

Prayer For The Day:

May we so love one another,
through You, Lord Jesus—that our homes
will be reflections of the glory of Your inestimable love.

·MAY 28·

"Every good gift and
every perfect gift is from above . . ."
James 1:17

God, in His mercy and goodness, has endowed every man with certain gifts, talents, and capabilities. These are not to be used selfishly for our own profit, but for the glory of God and for the building of His kingdom. Our personalities, our intelligence, and our capabilities are gifts from His own bountiful hand. If we divert their use for our own profit, we become guilty of selfishness. It is good business for an employee or junior partner in the firm to work for the profit and interest and glory of the owner. When the owner profits, all members of the firm profit. So, as stewards of our talents, we should invest them for the glory, praise, and honor of God. If God is glorified, we as His partners will be blessed. Our voices, our service, and our abilities are to be employed, primarily, for the glory of God.

Prayer For The Day:

Everything I have, You have given me, Father.
Now give me wisdom to use these gifts completely in Your will.

·MAY 29·

"For in him we
live and move and are!"
Acts 17:28 (TLB)

When I was seven years old, my father bought me my first bicycle. I had never ridden one. Patiently, my family and friends tried to teach me the art of cycling. I soon found out there was one thing I must do if I was to stay on the bicycle—keep moving forward. If I ceased to go forward, I would fall and hurt myself. So it is in the Christian life. We can never live this life on the highest plane unless we are continually growing and moving forward. You should be closer to God today in heart, soul, and body, than at any other time so far in your life.

Prayer For The Day:

Lord, I have progressed far
too slowly in my pilgrim walk with You.
Might I be drawn closer to the light of Your love and grace.

•MAY 30•

"Being justified freely by his grace
through the redemption that is in Christ Jesus."
Romans 3:24

S alvation is free! God puts no price tag on the Gift of gifts—it's free! Preachers are not salesmen, for they have nothing to sell. They are bearers of Good News—the good tidings that "Christ died for our sins according to the Scriptures" (1 Corinthians 15:3). Money can't buy it. Man's righteousness can't earn it. Social prestige can't help you acquire it. Morality can't purchase it. It is, as Isaiah said, "without money and without price." God is not a bargaining God. You cannot barter with Him. You must do business with Him on His own terms. He holds in His omnipotent hand the priceless, precious, eternal gift of salvation, and He bids you to take it without money and without price. The best things in life are free, are they not? The air we breathe is not sold by the cubic foot. The water which flows crystal clear from the mountain stream is free for the taking. Love is free, faith is free, hope is free.

Prayer For The Day:

Even though my salvation was
obtained only through the costliest sacrifice ever made,
You freely gave it to me. Lord, I praise You for this gift so lovingly
given.

• MAY 31 •

*"Therefore, if any man be in Christ,
he is a new creature: old things are passed
away; behold, all things are become new."*
2 Corinthians 5:17

The world says that all we need to do is be decent, respectable, and reasonable. True, that is all one needs to do to be a member of the Great Society, but to be a member of the Kingdom of God, there must be an inner change. A Communist in Hyde Park, London, pointed to a tramp and said, "Communism will put a new suit on that man." A Christian standing nearby said, "Yes, but Christ will put a new man in that suit!"

Prayer For The Day:

*Thank You, Lord Jesus, for
the change that came deep within me when I received You.*

• JUNE 1 •

*"This certain hope of being saved
is a strong and trustworthy anchor for our souls,
connecting us with God himself . . ."*
Hebrews 6:19 (TLB)

What are you placing your hope in for the future? Your country's government, educational system, some plan or organization? My hope is in a Person, the Lord Jesus Christ, who sits at the right hand of God. I have hope and know that I'm going to heaven. And, right here and now in this present life, I have God's presence to help me. Suppose we had no Bible. Suppose there were no cross, no salvation, no empty tomb. Suppose we had nothing to hang on to except, "Do your best, try to patch it up, do what you can." Oh, but we have a hope. There is a plan of redemption, a plan for the future. The New Testament is an exciting Book to read, it is so full of hope and expectancy. And God is interested in you!

Prayer For The Day:

*Reading Your Word, my heavenly Father,
makes me realize that the world and all its heartaches
is so transitory. Inspire me to reach others with Your message of
hope.*

·JUNE 2·

"If we are living now by
the Holy Spirit's power, let us follow the
Holy Spirit's leading in every
part of our lives."

Galatians 5:25 (TLB)

When Bill Borden, son of the wealthy Bordens, went out to China as a missionary, many of his friends thought he was foolish to "waste his life," as they put it, trying to convert a few heathens to Christianity. But Bill loved Christ and he loved men! He hadn't been out there very long before he contracted an oriental disease and died. At his bedside they found a note that he had written while he was dying. It read, "No reserve, no retreat, and no regrets." Bill had found more happiness in his few years of sacrificial service than most people find in a lifetime.

Prayer For The Day:

Help me not to count the cost of serving You,
Lord Jesus, but let me be completely yielded to Your leading.

·JUNE 3·

"Real life and real living
are not related to how rich we are."

Luke 12:15 (TLB)

There are two ways of being rich—have a lot, or want very little. The latter way is the easier for most of us. Many people make themselves miserable by wanting more than they can ever have. They suffer from "thing-itis," the insatiable desire for more, better, and newer things. Jesus was the most satisfied man that ever lived, and He had less than most of us. "The foxes have their holes, and the birds their nests, but the Son of man has no place to lay His head." He had learned the secret of adjusting His wants to His needs. E. Stanley Jones tells about a poor man who had an overnight guest, and as he showed him to his humble bedroom in the hayloft he said, "If there is anything you want, let us know, and we'll come and show you how to get along without it." We don't need to learn how to get more, but how to get along with what we've got, and get on with the business of living.

•JUNE 4•

*"Thus did Noah according
to all that God commanded him . . ."*
Genesis 6:22

O ne day God spoke to Noah about the wickedness of the human race. The actions of men and women grieved Him to the heart. God said that He intended to send a flood that would destroy mankind, and He told Noah to build an ark to save his household and the animals. The Bible says that Noah believed God. Now Noah had never seen a flood. He had never seen a 40-day rain. He had no weather map, no satellite photograph or meteorologist to tell him that a big storm was coming. All he had to go on was the Word of God. But when the flood came, Noah was spared and saved with his family, and the rest of the generation was swept away. Noah was saved because he put his trust in God. The days of Noah are returning to earth, and a catastrophe as great as the flood awaits those who refuse to enter into the ark of salvation, which is Jesus Christ.

Prayer For The Day:

*Forgive me, Father—so often I question, like Noah,
when I should be trusting You.*

•JUNE 5•

*"Stand steady, and don't be afraid of
suffering for the Lord.
Bring others to Christ . . ."*
2 Timothy 4:5 (TLB)

A ll the masterpieces of art contain both light and shadow. A happy life is one filled not only with sunshine, but one which uses both light and shadow to produce beauty. The greatest musicians, as a rule, are those who know how to bring song out of sadness. Fanny Crosby, her spirit aglow with faith in Christ, saw more with her sightless eyes than most of us do with normal vision.

She has given us some of the great gospel songs which cheer our hearts and lives. In a rat-infested jail in Philippi Paul and Silas sang their song of praise at midnight to the accompaniment of the jailer's whip. But their patience in suffering and persecution led to the heathen warden's conviction.

Prayer For The Day:

Let my heart learn to sing when
everything around me seems so dark.
Give me Your grace to praise You, Lord Jesus.

·JUNE 6·

". . . do the good things that result from
being saved, obeying God . . ."
Philippians 2:12 (TLB)

It takes no poll for those of us who have communicated with young people to know the devastation that permissive sexual activity generally causes. It becomes a cancer in the bodies and minds and characters of those who indulge, almost without exception. And there are other victims, such innocent bystanders as parents, grandparents, old family friends, teachers, and advisers, all much more concerned than you can understand. They want only the best for you. Anything less than a happy marital voyage gives them pain. The wisdom of their years says that premarital relations are always a mistake. The Bible teaches that God created sex. He made "male and female." Then it says, "God saw every thing that He had made, and behold, it was very good." This included the natural, sexual attraction between the man and woman He had created. Therefore, sex is not sin! It is God's gift to the human race. It is for procreation; for enjoyment within the bonds of matrimony; for the fulfillment of married love.

Prayer For The Day:

All the gifts You have given us are to be
enjoyed, within the structure of Your commandments,
heavenly Father. Keep me always conscious of Your teachings.

·JUNE 7·

"For if, when we were enemies,
we were reconciled to God by the
death of his Son . . ."

Romans 5:10

The word "reconcile" means literally "bring into a changed relationship." It means to bring together two parties who should have been together all along. The Bible speaks of the human race as enemies of God. You may say that you are no "enemy" of God, but according to Scripture we are either passive or active enemies of God, apart from Christ. Reconciliation means "brought back into full relationship and fellowship with God." This is what Christ accomplished on the cross. What a thrilling thought!

Prayer For The Day:

Your cross, dear Savior,
brings me to my knees in humble
gratitude. Thank You, for forgiving all the past
and giving me strength to live each day in Your power.

·JUNE 8·

"It is no shame to suffer for
being a Christian. Praise God for the privilege
of being in Christ's family and being
called by his wonderful name!"

1 Peter 4:16 (TLB)

A great problem in America is that we have an anemic and watered-down Christianity that has produced an anemic, watered-down, and spineless Christian who is not willing to stand up and be counted on every issue. We must have a virile, dynamic, aggressive Christian who lives Christ seven days a week, who is ready to die, if necessary, for his faith. We need Christians who are ethical, honest, gracious, bold, strong, and devoted followers of the Lord Jesus Christ.

Prayer For The Day:

I realize how spineless and pampered my Christian walk is.
Give me Your courage, Lord Jesus, to follow You more devotedly.

•JUNE 9•

"I was glad when they said unto me,
Let us go into the house of the Lord."

Psalm 122:1

A lot of people get what I call "Sunday-itis" on Sunday mornings. Do you know what Sunday-itis is? It attacks the victim shortly before breakfast on Sunday morning. It is accompanied by a feeling of weakness and lethargy. Sometimes the victim has a slight headache which is aggravated by the ringing of the church bells in the community. But the disease is of short duration, usually disappearing about noon, when the victim is able to eat a full dinner and play golf in the afternoon. But the symptoms usually appear again about 7:30 Sunday evening, and then disappear until the next Sunday morning.

Prayer For The Day:

May I always have the
gladness that David had, as each Sunday
I prepare to worship You in Your house, heavenly Father.

•JUNE 10•

". . . the love of God toward us . . ."

1 John 4:9

N otice God's love. The Bible teaches that God is love. You and I were sinners. We were aliens from God. We were enemies of God. We had rebelled against God. We deserved hell, but in spite of the fact that we resisted God, we rebelled against God, we sinned against God, we were enemies of God—the Bible says God loved us anyway with an everlasting love so that He was willing to give His Son to die on the cross for our sins. There is not a person who has the ability to love that way unless he comes to Christ. You don't have the power to love.

Prayer For The Day:

Your love encompasses me,
Lord Jesus, wherever I may be. There are
so many who need the healing of Your love in
their lives. Fill me to overflowing with "agapē" love for them.

·JUNE 11·

"Behold, what manner of love the
Father hath bestowed upon us, that we should
be called the [children] of God . . ."

1 John 3:1

As God's children, we are His dependents. The Bible says, "Like as a father pitieth his children, so the Lord pitieth them that fear Him." Dependent children spend little time worrying about meals, clothing, and shelter. They assume, and they have a right to, that all will be provided by their parents. Because God is responsible for our welfare, we are told to cast all our care upon Him, for He careth for us. Because we are dependent upon God, Jesus said, "Let not your heart be troubled." God says, "I'll take care of the burden—don't give it a thought—leave it to me." Dependent children are not backward about asking for favors. They would not be normal if they did not boldly make their needs known. God is keenly aware that we are dependent upon Him for life's necessities. It was for that reason that He said, "Ask, and it shall be given you; seek, and ye shall find; knock, and it shall be opened unto you."

Prayer For The Day:

How magnificent, almighty Father,
that I, dependently, can rely
on You to take the burden of my heart!

·JUNE 12·

"Commit thy way unto the Lord;
trust also in him; and he shall
bring it to pass."

Psalm 37:5

To know the will of God is the highest of all wisdom. Living in the center of God's will rules out all falseness of religion and puts the stamp of true sincerity upon our service to God. You can be miserable with much, if you are out of His will; but you can have peace in your heart with little, if you are in the will of God. You can be wretched with wealth and fame, out of His will; but you can have joy in obscurity, if you are in the will of God. You can have agony in good health, out of His will; but you can be happy in the midst of suffering, if you are in God's will. You can be miserable and defeated in the midst of acclaim, if you are out of His will; but you can be calm and at peace in the midst of persecution, as long as you are in the will of God. The Bible reveals that God has a plan for every life, and that if we live in constant fellowship with Him, He will direct and lead us in the fulfillment of this plan.

Prayer For The Day:

In everything I do, Your will must be
uppermost in my life, Lord. I, as Your child, trust You to lead me.

•JUNE 13•

". . . I [have] raised thee up,
that I might shew my power in thee . . ."
Romans 9:17

Walter Knight tells the story about a little boy who had recently received Christ. "Daddy, how can I believe in the Holy Spirit when I have never seen Him?" asked Jim. "I'll show you how," said his father, who was an electrician. Later Jim went with his father to the power plant where he was shown the generators. "This is where the power comes from to heat our stove and to give us light. We cannot see the power, but it is in that machine and in the power lines," said the father. "I believe in electricity," said Jim. "Of course you do," said his father, "but you don't believe in it because you see it. You believe in it because you see what it can do. Likewise, you can believe in the Holy Spirit because you can see what He does in people's lives when they are surrendered to Christ and possess His power."

Prayer For The Day:

Make my heart completely devoid of
self so that it can be filled with Your Spirit, Lord.

·JUNE 14·

"... for they have
rejected the word of the Lord ..."
Jeremiah 8:9 (TLB)

T he Apostle Paul once asked, "Who art thou, Lord?" That is a question each of us has to face. If Jesus claimed to be the Son of God, knowing He was not, then He was a deceiver, the greatest liar the world has ever known. If He thought He was God and didn't know the difference, then He was a mental case. But if He was who He claimed to be, then He is rightfully the Lord of our lives. What keeps us from acknowledging this Christ, if He is what the Bible tells us He is? Each of us has to face the question that Pilate asked, "What shall I do then with Jesus which is called the Christ?" Pilate washed his hands and said he would have nothing to do with Jesus, but God does not let us off that way. We must say "yes" or "no." We can make fun of Jesus, we can reject Him, we can neglect Him—or we can receive Him.

Prayer For The Day:

Lord Jesus, with so many still
rejecting You, take away everything within
me that would stop another receiving You as Savior and Lord.

·JUNE 15·

"Redeeming the time ..."
Ephesians 5:16

W e are stewards of our time. God has given each one of us a little "chunk of eternity" called time. These golden moments of opportunity are doled out to us for our benefit and for God's glory. If we use them wisely, they are woven by God's omnipotent hand into the fabric of eternity. Henry Thoreau cautioned, "You cannot kill time without injuring eternity." "He who has no vision of eternity," said Carlyle, "has no hold on time." "Only one life, 'twill soon be past; only what's done for Christ will last" is the sentiment of every man who desires to be a good steward of his time. We are entrusted with a small portion of the capital of time. If we invest it wisely, it will pay dividends throughout eternity.

• JUNE 16 •

*"Open my eyes to see
wonderful things in your Word."*
Psalm 119:18 (TLB)

S ome, who doubt that the Bible is the true Word of God, doubt it because they are unwilling to ascribe to God anything they cannot themselves achieve. If you have any uncertainty about the inspiration of the Bible, go back and look at it again. Look at it in the light of a person who has been staring at a mud puddle all his life, and who is confronted for the first time by a view of the ocean! Perhaps you are only now catching your first glimpse of God's un-limited power. Perhaps you are only now beginning to understand Him for what He actually is. For if God is the Spirit that Jesus declares Him to be, there is no problem of providence, there is no problem of His sovereignty in the affairs of men, there is no prob-lem of His inspiration of the men who wrote the Bible. Everything fits into place, once you understand who and what God really is.

Prayer For The Day:

*My Father and my God,
as I read the Scriptures each day,
You open my eyes to more of the glories of Your wondrous love.*

• JUNE 17 •

*"Those who still reject me are like
the restless sea. . . . There is no
peace, says my God, for them!"*
Isaiah 57:20,21 (TLB)

F aith has legs . . . I heard about a man some years ago who was rolling a wheelbarrow back and forth on a tightrope across Niagara River. Thousands of people were shouting him on. He put a 200-pound sack of dirt in the wheelbarrow and rolled it over, and then he rolled it back. He turned to the crowd and asked, "How many of you believe that I can roll a man across?" Everybody shouted! One man in the front row was very excited in his professed belief. The man pointed to this excited professor and said, "You're next!" You couldn't see that man for dust! He didn't actually believe it. He thought he believed it—but he was not willing to get in the wheelbarrow. Just so with Christ. Many people say they believe on Him, they say they follow Him. But they never have stepped into the wheelbarrow. They actually never have committed and surrendered themselves wholly, 100 percent to Christ.

Prayer For The Day:

Loving Lord Jesus, it was only
when I surrendered everything to You that
I knew the ultimate joy and peace that had always escaped me.

•JUNE 18•

"What a wonderful God we have . . .
who so wonderfully comforts and strengthens us
. . ."
2 Corinthians 1:3,4 (TLB)

T he Bible teaches unmistakably that we can triumph over bereavement. The Psalmist said, "Weeping may endure for a night, but joy cometh in the morning." Self-pity can bring no enduring comfort. The fact is, it will only add to your misery. And unremitting grief will give you little consolation in itself, for grief begets grief. Sorrow, or mourning, when it is borne in a Christian way, contains a built-in comfort. "Happy are they that mourn; for they shall be comforted." There is comfort in mourning, because we know that Christ is with us. He has said, "Lo, I am with you alway, even unto the end of the world." Suffering is endurable if we do not have to bear it alone; and the more compassionate the Presence, the less acute the pain.

Prayer For The Day:

Thank You, loving heavenly Father,
for the promise that when we mourn
You will comfort us. I have felt the healing of
Your consolation in the past and know You will never fail me.

·JUNE 19·

"... set your sights on the
rich treasures and joys of heaven ..."
Colossians 3:1 (TLB)

Have you ever been separated from someone you love? A boy-friend or girl friend whom you have not seen in three or four months? Wait until you see each other! My wife and I have said goodbyes to each other; but when we meet, it's a honeymoon all over again. And that is what it will be like on that glorious day when Jesus Christ comes. We will be caught up in the air to meet Him, and it will be like two lovers coming together. What hope we have!

Prayer For The Day:

Lord Jesus, when You come again,
how many hearts will rejoice. Until then,
with expectant anticipation I eagerly wait for that glorious day!

·JUNE 20·

"If we confess our sins, he is
faithful and just to forgive us our sins, and to
cleanse us from all unrighteousness."
1 John 1:9

It is unfortunate in a marriage if there is an array of sordid mem-ories of past sins on the part of either partner. If young people could only realize that a happy marriage depends not only on the present, but upon the past, they would be more reluctant to enter into loose, intimate relations with anyone and everyone. Many a marriage has been imperiled by the backlash of past sins, which were not just confessed, but "found out." As to the necessity of confessing past sins to one's mate, I don't think this is always advis-able or necessary. I have known of homes that were wrecked by such confessions. The main thing is to confess any past wrongs to God, resolve to be true to your marriage vows; and absolve the black past by a spotless present.

Prayer For The Day:

Thank You for forgiving and forgetting
the past. Help me to do the same, Lord.

·JUNE 21·

*"Now change your mind and attitude
to God and turn to him so he can cleanse away
your sins and send you wonderful times
of refreshment from the presence of the Lord."*
Acts 3:19 (TLB)

There is a certain amount of sorrow involved in repentance that we don't see much of today. That word means moaning and even groaning. I don't mean that we have to have a great emotional experience, but I do believe that we need some tears of repentance. We need to be sorry for our sins, and to say, "Oh, God, I have sinned against You, and I'm sorry." I am not an emotional person. I don't know why, but I don't cry easily. But of the few times I have cried in my life, some of them have been over sin that I committed many years ago. The night I came to Christ, I didn't have any tears. But later I went home and I looked out my window at the North Carolina sky and I cried over my sins. I said, "Oh, God, forgive me." And the most wonderful peace swept over my soul. From that moment on, I've known that my sins were forgiven.

Prayer For The Day:

*There is sorrow in my soul when I
remember how I fail You, loving Lord. Forgive my frailties.*

·JUNE 22·

*"Worthy is the Lamb . . . to receive
power, and riches, and wisdom, and strength,
and honor, and glory, and blessing."*
Revelation 5:12

H. G. Wells wrote, "Christ is the most unique person of history. No man can write a history of the human race without giving first and foremost place to the penniless teacher of Nazareth." Rabbi Stephen Wise said concerning Jesus, "You will find that He is divinely human. It is no mean joy to us of the house of Israel to recognize, to honor and to cherish among our brethren, Jesus the Jew, who has influenced the world more than any other man." This person called Jesus lived on earth for only 33 years. He never traveled more than 100 miles from His home. Yet Charles

Lamb was right in saying, "If all the illustrious men of history were gathered together and Shakespeare should enter their presence, they would rise to do him honor; but if Jesus Christ should come in, they would fall down and worship Him."

Prayer For The Day:

*Loving Lord Jesus, I would
honor You this day and evermore—
in adoration I worship You, my Savior and my Lord.*

•JUNE 23•

*"God did not send his Son into the
world to condemn it, but to save it."*

John 3:17 (TLB)

You can put a public school and university in the middle of every block of every city in America—but you will never keep America from rotting morally by mere intellectual education. Education cannot be properly called education which neglects the most important parts of man's nature. Partial education throughout the world is far worse than none at all if we educate the mind but not the soul. To think of civilizing men without converting them to Christ is about as wise as to think about transforming wolves into lambs merely by washing them and putting on them a fleece of wool. "Happy are the merciful: for they shall obtain mercy." The mercy the world needs is the grace, love, and peace of our Lord Jesus Christ. It is His transforming and regenerating power that the world needs more than anything else.

Prayer For The Day:

*Merciful Lord, may my life be filled
with Your outflowing love for others.*

·JUNE 24·

"The wisdom that is from above is
first pure, then peaceable, gentle, and easy to
be intreated, full of mercy and good fruits,
without partiality, and without hypocrisy."

James 3:17

T he world, in the last few years, has reverted to a sort of bar-
barism. As practical Christianity has declined, rudeness and
violence have increased. Neighbors quarrel with neighbors. Fighting
is a major problem in our schools and the "gang wars" of the teen-
agers have come to present a serious menace in our cities. Fathers
and mothers wrangle and bicker. Homes are disintegrating. High
government officials in Washington engage in name-calling and in
heated disputes not at all in keeping with the dignity of their office.
Why and how has all this savagery crept into our social life? It is
because we have forgotten Jesus' words, "Happy are the meek; for
they shall inherit the earth." I have seen tough, rough, hardened
men open their hearts by faith, receive Christ as Savior, and become gentle, patient, merciful gentlemen.

Prayer For The Day:

Fill me with Your mercy and love, Lord.
In an angry world let me be used to bring peace where there is
strife.

B's Birthday
1952

·JUNE 25·

"And the Lord said, Who then
is that faithful and wise steward . . . ?"

Luke 12:42

I t is not wrong for men to possess riches. But the Bible warns that
money cannot buy happiness! Money cannot buy true pleasure.
Money cannot buy peace of heart. And money certainly cannot
buy entrance into the Kingdom of God. Often money is a hin-
drance to these things. Money takes our minds off God. Riches,
when used selfishly rather than for the glory of God, tend to cor-
rupt in our hands. Money cannot be a substitute for God. If God
has given you more wealth than your neighbors, dedicate it to
Christ. Realize that you are only a steward of that which God has
given you and some day you will have to give an account of every

penny you have spent. The Internal Revenue Service wants a record of how you spend your money, but that is nothing compared to the books God is keeping.

Prayer For The Day:

> *Father, I would be a faithful steward of all You have given to me. Make me constantly aware of Your leading so I may wisely spend any money with which I have been entrusted.*

·JUNE 26·

> *"You are controlled by your new nature if you have the Spirit of God living in you . . ."*
> Romans 8:9 (TLB)

A harnessed horse contributes much more to life than a wild donkey. Energy out of control is dangerous; energy under control is powerful. God does not discipline us to subdue us, but to condition us for a life of usefulness and blessedness. In His wisdom He knows that an uncontrolled life is an unhappy life, so He puts reins on our wayward souls that they may be directed into the "paths of righteousness." That is what God seeks to do with us; to tame us, to bring us under proper control, to redirect our energies. He does in the spiritual realm what science does in the physical realm. Science takes a Niagara River with its violent turbulence and transforms it into electrical energy to illuminate a million homes and to turn the productive wheels of industry.

Prayer For The Day:

> *Direct all my energy, Father, so that I may be a blessing to others.*

•JUNE 27•

"What a glorious Lord!
He who daily bears our burdens
also gives us our salvation."
Psalm 68:19 (TLB)

E dward Dahlberg, the writer, observed, "At nineteen, I was a stranger to myself. At forty, I asked, 'Who am I?' At fifty, I concluded I would never know." This unexplored personal wilderness is the home of millions of people. Ninety-two percent of all Canadian university students, according to June Callwood, the Toronto sociologist, don't really know who they are. The Bible says that man is an immortal soul. When God made man in the first place, He created him and "breathed into his nostrils the breath of life; and man became a living soul" (Genesis 2:7). One's soul is the essence, the core, the eternal and real person. And he will be restless until he opens his life to Jesus Christ as Savior and Lord.

Prayer For The Day:

Almighty God, knowing I am
Your child is all the assurance I need.

•JUNE 28•

"And when he was in
affliction, he besought the Lord his God,
and humbled himself . . ."
2 Chronicles 33:12

W hy do Christians suffer? Rest assured that there is a reason for Christian people being afflicted. One reason why God's people suffer, according to the Bible, is that it is a disciplinary, chastening, and molding process. From the Scriptures we learn that the chastening of affliction is a step in the process of our full and complete development. Affliction can also be a means of refining and of purification. Many a life has come forth from the furnace of affliction more beautiful and more useful than before.

Prayer For The Day:

Lord, whatever I have to face,
through it let me learn more of Your love and compassion.

·JUNE 29·

"... I was hungry, [and] you gave me food ..."
Matthew 25:35 (NEB)

During the war a church in Strasburg, Germany, was totally destroyed; but a statue of Christ which stood by the altar was almost unharmed. Only the hands of the statue were missing. When the church was rebuilt, a famous sculptor offered to make new hands; but, after considering the matter, the members decided to let it stand as it was—without hands. "For," they said, "Christ has no hands but our hands to do His work on earth. If we don't feed the hungry, give drink to the thirsty, entertain the stranger, visit the imprisoned, and clothe the naked, who will?" Christ is depending on us to do the very things which He did while upon earth. My friend, if the gospel we preach does not have a social application, if it will not work effectively in the work-a-day world, then it is not the Gospel of Jesus Christ.

Prayer For The Day:

I look at my hands, Lord Jesus, and
ask You to use them this day.
Make me conscious of the needs of those who hurt.

·JUNE 30·

"And all things, whatever ye shall
ask in prayer, believing, ye shall receive."
Matthew 21:22

Prayer is a two-way conversation; it is our talking to God, and His talking to us. As a Christian, you have a heavenly Father who hears and answers prayer. Jesus said, "All things, whatsoever ye shall ask in prayer, believing, ye shall receive." Every man or woman whose life has counted for the church and the Kingdom of God has been a person of prayer. You cannot afford to be too busy to pray. A prayerless Christian is a powerless Christian. Jesus Christ spent many hours in prayer. Sometimes He spent the night on a mountaintop in solitary communion with God the Father. If He felt that He had to pray, how much more do we need to pray!

Prayer For The Day:

There is inexpressible joy as
I come to You in prayer, my heavenly Father.

• JULY 1 •

"His every word is a
treasure of knowledge and understanding."
Proverbs 2:6 (TLB)

I t is small wonder . . . the Bible has always been the world's best seller! No other book can touch its profound wisdom, its poetic beauty, or the accuracy of its history and prophecy. Its critics who claimed it to be filled with forgery, fiction, and unfulfilled promises, are finding that the difficulties lie with themselves, and not the Bible. Greater and more careful scholarship has shown that apparent contradictions were caused by incorrect translations, rather than divine inconsistencies. It was man and not the Bible that needed correcting. And yet—in many homes and among so-called educated people—it has become fashionable to joke about the Bible and to regard it more as a dust-catcher than as the living Word of God. . . . Too many families have used the Bible as a safe storage place for old letters and pressed flowers, and have overlooked entirely the help and assurance that God intended this Book to give them.

Prayer For The Day:

Almighty God, I praise You for the authority
of Your Word, which speaks to me of my redemption,
life as it should be lived, peace and eternal life with You.

• JULY 2 •

"Love one another,
as I have loved you."
John 15:12

A s I study the subject of "separation" in the Old and New Testaments, I discover that the weight of Scripture lies in the direction of fellowship rather than separation. What is the great overwhelming evidence that we have passed from death unto life? It is love! Jesus Christ clearly was speaking of visible unity, such as can be seen by the world. His motive for praying was that the world might believe and the world might know. He prayed for unity among believers. God, who wills man's unity in Christ, is a God of variety. So often we want everyone to be the same—to think and speak and believe as we do. Many Scripture passages could be called to witness that love is the real key to Christian unity. In the spirit of true humility, compassion, consideration, and unselfishness, we are to approach our problems, our work, and even our differences.

Prayer For The Day:

In a world needing Your love, let me not judge those
who love You too. You have made us all so different, Father.
Teach me, by Your loving Holy Spirit, compassion and true unity.

•JULY 3•

"All scripture is given by inspiration
of God, and is profitable . . ."

2 Timothy 3:16

The men who framed our Constitution knew they were writing the basic document for a government of free men; they recognized that men could live as free and independent beings only if each one knew and understood the law. They were to know their rights, their privileges, and their limitations. They were to stand as equals before the court of law, and few judges could be unfair; for the judge, too, was bound by the same law and required to try each case accordingly. . . . As the Constitution is the highest law of the land, so the Bible is the highest law of God. For it is in the Bible that God sets forth His spiritual laws. It is in the Bible that God makes His enduring promises. It is in the Bible that God reveals the plan of redemption for the human race.

Prayer For The Day:

Almighty God, each day our nation
and we, the people, face so many crises.
May each one of us seek wisdom through Your Word, the Bible.

•JULY 4•

"Fear God and honor the government . . ."
1 Peter 2:17 (TLB)

On this Independence Day we should be on our knees thanking God for all He has given us. The United States is a country in which everyone has an equal opportunity. Thank God for a country where there is no caste or class to keep a man from going to the top. If a man has a will to work and study, he can go ahead regardless of his background. In addition, thank God, He has given us freedom of religion. Whatever you may believe, no one can close your church because your religion does not coincide with his. A few people meeting in a small, out-of-the-way shack, worshiping God as they believe in Him, have the same right to religious freedom as the people who worship God in the great cathedrals on the avenues of our greatest cities.

Prayer For The Day:

Thank You, God, for allowing me to live in the
greatest, grandest, and most free land the world has ever known.

•JULY 5•

"The law of the Lord is perfect . . ."
Psalm 19:7

The Bible is the constitution of Christianity. Just as the United States Constitution is not of any private interpretation, neither is the Bible of any private interpretation. Just as the Constitution includes all who live under its stated domain, without exception, so the Bible includes all who live under its stated domain, without exception. God's laws for the spiritual world are found in the Bible. Whatever else there may be that tells us of God, it is more clearly told in the Bible. Nature in her laws tells us of God, but the message is not too clear. It tells us nothing of the love and grace of God. Conscience, in our inmost being, does tell us of God, but the message is fragmentary. The only place we can find a clear, unmistakable message is in the Word of God, which we call the Bible.

Prayer For The Day:

How I pray that the world would live by Your law—
which bears no discrimination but is perfect.
Teach me as I read the Bible to follow Your commandments—
which are not impossible to obey because of Jesus Christ's love.

•JULY 6•

*"These things I have spoken unto you,
that in me ye might have peace. In the world ye shall
have tribulation: but be of good cheer;
I have overcome the world."*

John 16:33

The peace that Jesus came to bring was not the peace of appeasement, or the peace of compromise and conformity. It was a spiritual peace. The world doesn't give peace, for it doesn't have any peace to give. It fights for peace, it negotiates for peace, it maneuvers for peace, but there is no ultimate peace in the world. But Jesus gives peace to those who put their trust in Him. If you have received His peace, then you are in His camp. But if you have rejected it, then you are against Him. His peace is available to everyone who will receive it.

Prayer For The Day:

*Deep down I feel Your peace,
Lord Jesus, and the storms of my life are abated.*

•JULY 7•

*"Yea, the Lord shall give
that which is good; and our land
shall yield her increase."*

Psalm 85:12

The great economic and material prosperity we are enjoying in the United States today is a gift of God's hand. The Bible tells us that the very goodness of God should lead us to repentance. All of these material blessings are gifts from God, given in order that we might humble ourselves, fall upon our knees before Him, and call upon His name. We should thank God, too, for the spiritual blessings that are beyond the power of human tongue to describe. Here in North America we still have freedom of worship. In many parts of the world believers cannot assemble together; they cannot speak of their religious convictions because of totalitarian power. Here in North America we have Bibles everywhere. We have the opportunity to preach. God has blessed us with a thousand and one spiritual blessings. In days of uncertainty and confusion, such as we are now passing through, these are gifts that go beyond our power to understand; and yet they are gifts of God that become ours when we receive His Son as our Savior and Lord.

Prayer For The Day:

*Almighty God, I thank You for
all the blessings You shower upon this
land—and I would thank You especially for my freedom
to worship You and read my Bible, without fear of persecution.*

⋅JULY 8⋅

"He must increase, but I must decrease."
                                        John 3:30

Self-centeredness is the basic cause of much of our distress in life. Hypochondria, a mental disorder which is accompanied by melancholy and depression, is often caused by self-pity and self-centeredness. Most of us suffer from spiritual nearsightedness. Our interests, our loves, and our energies are too often focused upon ourselves. Jesus underscored the fact that His disciples were to live outflowingly rather than selfishly. To the rich young ruler He said, "If thou wilt be perfect, go and sell that thou hast, and give to the poor, and thou shalt have treasure in heaven" (Matthew 19:21). It wasn't the giving away of his goods that Jesus demanded, particularly, but that he be released from selfishness, and its devastating effect on his personality and life.

Prayer For The Day:

*Teach me to so completely open my
heart to You there will be no room for self.
Cleanse me, Lord, of all selfish thoughts and deeds.*

⋅JULY 9⋅

*"May my spoken words and
unspoken thoughts be pleasing even to you,
O Lord my Rock and my Redeemer."*
                                        Psalm 19:14 (TLB)

Robert Browning said, "Thought is the soul of the act." Emerson said, "Thought is the seat of action. The ancestor of every action is thought." If God destroyed the world once for its continually evil imaginations, is it not reasonable to believe that all of the sin, lust, and licentiousness that is rampant today grieves His heart just as it did in that day? Many people dream of sin, imagine sin, and—if granted the opportunity—would indulge in sin. All they lack is the occasion to sin. So, in the sight of God, they are sinners as great as though they actually had committed immorality. All transgressions begin with sinful thinking. You who have come to Christ for a pure heart, guard against the pictures of lewdness and sensuality which Satan flashes upon the screen of your imagination, select with care the books you read, choose discerningly the kind of entertainment you attend, the kind of associates with whom you mingle, and the kind of environment in which you place yourself. You should no more allow sinful imaginations to accumulate in your mind and soul than you would let garbage collect in your living room.

Prayer For The Day:

I need my thoughts to be continually
purified by the cleansing power of Your Spirit, almighty God.

•JULY 10•

"Do not be anxious for your life . . ."
Matthew 6:25 (NASB)

S ome people ask, "Do you think God has time for me? You don't know how mixed up my life is, how confused it is; the pressures, the tension at home, the business problems, so many things I couldn't possibly tell you about, including the sins in my life that I somehow cannot seem to give up." Yes, God has time for you. When Jesus was dying on the cross, He had time for a thief who turned to Him and said, "Lord, remember me." That's all the record tells us that the thief said, "Lord, remember me." But what he was really saying was, "I'm unworthy. I've broken all the laws. I deserve hell. Just remember me." And Jesus turned to him in that moment and said, "Today you will be with me in Paradise."

Prayer For The Day:

Even in Your greatest suffering, Lord Jesus,
You had time to assure another of Your love.
My heart is comforted to know this caring for my soul is infinite.

•JULY 11•

"Looking for that blessed hope . . ."
Titus 2:13

One of the best ways to get rid of discouragement is to remember that Christ is coming again. The most thrilling, glorious truth in all the world is the Second Coming of Jesus Christ. When we look around and see pessimism on every side, we should remember the Bible is the only Book in the world that predicts the future. The Bible is more modern than tomorrow morning's newspaper. The Bible accurately foretells the future, and it says that the consummation of all things shall be the coming again of Jesus Christ to this earth. If your life is dismal, depressed, and gloomy today, Christ can turn those dark clouds inside out. The sunlight of His love can still shine into the darkest part of your life.

Prayer For The Day:

Longing to see Your face, Christ Jesus,
I rejoice in the anticipation of Your coming again!

•JULY 12•

"Jesus saith . . .
I am the way, the truth, and the life . . ."
John 14:6

With much of society a disappointment, young people have begun to search for answers on their own. Everywhere I travel, I find young people who are asking: What is truth? Who says so? What is right and what is wrong? Is there a final authority? Yes! There is an authority! There is a moral law! It has been exemplified in a real Person. There is a genuine Hero in whom you can believe, who will never let you down. His name is Jesus Christ. He was born into a world as jumbled and riddled with injustice as yours, but He changed it by changing people.

Prayer For The Day:

You, Lord Jesus, are the
Supreme Authority; and my soul praises You!

•JULY 13•

*"The Lord hath anointed me . . . to
proclaim liberty to the captives, and the
opening of the prison
to those who are bound."*

Isaiah 61:1

V iktor Frankl in his book, *Man's Search for Meaning*, describes the reactions of two brothers with the same heredity, the same environment, in the same concentration camp under the Nazis. One became a saint and the other a swine. Frankl tells us the reason why. He said, "Each man has within him the power to choose how he will react to any given situation." God has given us the power of choice. Some people today do not wish to accept the responsibility for their actions. They blame society. They blame the environment. They blame the schools. They blame the circumstances. But Adam sinned in a perfect environment under perfect circumstances. We can't blame it all on somebody else. We must accept the blame ourselves for our part. Society is made up of individuals. If we have social injustice, we're the ones who are wrong; we're part of it. Let's accept our responsibility to do something about it.

Prayer For The Day:

*With Your help, living Lord,
I want to make the right decisions so
that I may touch society with Your healing love.*

•JULY 14•

*"Follow not that which
is evil, but that which is good . . ."*

3 John 11

W e must get this fact firmly fixed in our minds: we live in an upside-down world. People hate when they should love, quarrel when they should be friendly, fight when they should be peaceful, wound when they should heal, steal when they should share, do wrong when they should do right. I once saw a toy clown with a weight in its head. No matter what position you put it in, it invariably assumed an upside-down position. Put it on its feet or on its side, and when you let go it flipped back on its head. Unregenerate people are just like that! Do what you may with them and they always revert to an upside-down position. That is why the disciples to the world were misfits. To an upside-down person, a right-side up person seems upside down. To a sinner, a righteous person is an oddity and an abnormality. A Christian's goodness is a rebuke to the wicked; his being right-side up is a reflection upon the worldling's inverted position.

Prayer For The Day:

> *Let me never compromise my stand for You,*
> *Lord Jesus, who gave Your sinless life for me.*

•JULY 15•

"They shall see his face . . ."
Revelation 22:4 (TLB)

One of the great bonuses of being a Christian is the great hope that extends beyond the grave into the glory of God's to-morrow. A little girl was running toward the cemetery as the dark-ness of evening began to fall. She passed a friend who asked her if she was not afraid to go through the graveyard at night. "Oh, no," she said, "I'm not afraid. My home is just on the other side!" We Christians are not afraid of the night of death because our heavenly home is "just on the other side." The resurrection of Christ changed the midnight of bereavement into a sunrise of reunion; it changed the midnight of disappointment into a sunrise of joy; it changed the midnight of fear to a sunrise of peace. Today faith and confidence in the resurrected Christ can change your fear to hope and your disappointment to joy.

Prayer For The Day:

> *Whatever I fear the most, Lord Jesus, I put into*
> *Your loving hands, knowing You will give me peace and courage.*

•JULY 16•

"Lord, grant us peace; for
all we have and are has come from you."
Isaiah 26:12 (TLB)

Only a few years ago children were delighted at the prospect of a trip to the wharves to see the great ships come in. Today they are blasé about helicopters and jet planes. We who once marveled at the telegraph now take for granted the far greater miracle of television. Not so long ago many of the physical diseases were termed hopeless and incurable. Today we have drugs so effective that age-old diseases are becoming rare. We have accomplished much, of that there is no doubt. But with all this progress, we have not solved the basic problem of the human race. We can build the highest buildings, the fastest ships, the longest bridges—but we still can't govern ourselves, or live together peacefully and with equality.

Prayer For The Day:

In loving and being loved by You,
there is all I have longed for, my Savior, Jesus Christ.

•JULY 17•

"God is our refuge and strength,
a tested help in times of trouble."
Psalm 46:1 (TLB)

Scripture tells us that God tempts no one. Temptation always comes from the devil. God will test us and allow us to endure the temptation, but the devil does the tempting. How do we overcome it? A little girl once told her method. "When the devil comes knocking at the door," she said, "I don't answer it. I send Jesus to the door." And that is exactly the way to take care of it. Send Jesus to the door!

Prayer For The Day:

Lord Jesus, help me
to remember the power of Your holy name!

•JULY 18•

"Thou shalt rejoice
in every good thing which the Lord thy God
hath given unto thee . . ."
Deuteronomy 26:11

Often the Church has banged away negatively at evils without reminding us that God is tremendously interested in our finding a satisfying way of life here and now. We Christians have talked so much of the negative side of Christian experience that we have forgotten to emphasize the positive, joyous, thrilling, and victorious experience of daily fellowship with Christ. God declared that *things* will not satisfy. God satisfies! This is the secret of soul-satisfaction: Let your soul delight itself in fatness. Remove the obstructions, tear down the barriers, and let your soul find the fulfillment of its deepest longings in fellowship with God.

Prayer For The Day:

There are no words to describe
my gratitude to You, my Lord and Savior,
for Your loving kindness. Accept my praise and love.

•JULY 19•

"Not by might, nor by power,
but by my Spirit, says the Lord of Hosts . . ."
Zechariah 4:6 (TLB)

After the crucifixion the beleaguered disciples despaired and said, "We had hoped that He was the one to redeem Israel" (Luke 24:21, RSV). There was anguish, despair, and tragedy in their midst. Life had lost its meaning and purpose. But when the resurrection became apparent, life took on a new meaning. It had purpose and reason. David Livingstone once addressed a group of students at Glasgow University. When he rose to speak, he bore on his body the marks of his African struggles. Several illnesses on nearly 30 occasions had left him gaunt and haggard. His left arm, crushed by a lion, hung limp by his side. After describing his trials and tribulations he said, "Would you like to have me tell you what supported me through all the years of exile among people whose language I could not understand, and whose attitude toward me was always uncertain and often hostile? It was this, 'Lo, I am with you alway, even unto the end of the world.' On these words I staked everything, and they never failed."

Prayer For The Day:

*I am never alone because
of Your love. Thank You, my Lord and Savior.*

•JULY 20•

*"Thanks be unto God
for his unspeakable gift."*
2 Corinthians 9:15

A gift is not a gift unless it is accepted. God has given you His Son, but ownership is conditional on acceptance. God does not force His gift on us, but He asks us to receive by faith the gift of His Son, Jesus Christ. A person who deliberately refuses God's offer of love, mercy, and forgiveness is lost. Most people gratefully receive a gift when given in love. The greatest sin that a person can commit is to refuse God's love.

Prayer For The Day:

*I reached out for Your gift
of Jesus and received forgiveness and
eternal life. Thank You, my heavenly Father.*

•JULY 21•

*"Except your righteousness shall
exceed the righteousness of the scribes and
Pharisees, ye shall in no case
enter into the kingdom of heaven."*
Matthew 5:20

In a decadent society the will to believe, to resist, to contend, to fight, to struggle, is gone. In place of this will to resist, there is the desire to conform, to drift, to follow, to yield, and to give up. This is what happened in Rome, but it also applies to us. The same conditions that prevailed in Rome prevail in our society. Before Rome fell, her standards were abandoned, the family disintegrated, divorce prevailed, immorality was rampant, and faith was at a low ebb. As Gibbon said, "There was much talk of religion, but few practiced it."

Prayer For The Day:

May I be worthy to bear the name Christian, Lord Jesus.

•JULY 22•

"Being justified by faith, we have
peace with God through our Lord Jesus Christ."
                                                    Romans 5:1

Before the Big Four Conference in Geneva I watched President Eisenhower kneel in a chapel and ask God for divine guidance in the deliberations to follow. I felt sure that God would answer his earnest prayer. I believe that He did, for President Eisenhower during those days displayed the spirit of a true peacemaker on the international level. The only corrective measure in establishing peace is for men as individuals to know the peace of God. Though I am not wholly averse to movements which strive in one way or another for world peace, I have a strong conviction that such peace will never come unless there is a spiritual dynamic at the core. I pray for wars to cease, just as I pray for crime to stop; but I know that the basic cause of both crime and war is the inherent sinfulness of human nature. The world cannot be reborn until men are born again and are at peace with God.

Prayer For The Day:

Heavenly Father, I pray for the peace of
the world through individuals surrendering to Your Son, Jesus
Christ.
Bless all today who are spreading the Gospel here and abroad.

•JULY 23•

"I am with you, that is all you need.
My power shows up best in weak people."
                                          2 Corinthians 12:9 (TLB)

A director of a camp whose purpose is to lead young hoodlums to Christ says, "Being a Christian is the toughest thing in the world. What's tougher than loving your enemy?" One boy, who developed into a rugged disciple of Christ at this camp, said, "In this outfit we're all brothers and we're all men. It was too tough for me at first, but then I heard that through Christ everything is possible. Then the roughness went away. I say a man is not a man, not a full man, until he gets to know Jesus Christ." Yes, the Christian life is tough and rough; but it's challenging. It's worth everything it costs to be a follower of Jesus Christ. You will soon find that the cross is not greater than His grace. When you pick up the cross of unpopularity, wherever you may be, you will find God's grace is there, more than sufficient to meet your every need.

Prayer For The Day:

Lord Jesus, teach me the lesson that
Your grace is abundantly sufficient to meet my every need.

•JULY 24•

Gene's Bday
1926

> *"He that is faithful in that which*
> *is least is faithful also in much . . ."*
>
> *Luke 16:10*

W hat God expects, and all God expects, is that we dedicate completely all of our talents and gifts to Him. That is the meaning of the parable of the talents in Matthew, chapter 25. Read this parable, and you will see that we are always rewarded because of our faithfulness. You can be just as faithful as anyone and have the commendation of the Lord. Take the one talent you have and invest it in eternal things. Some talented people lose their reward because they do things to be seen of men. Some untalented people lose their reward because they fail to dedicate what they have, because it is not noticed by men. Both have sinned equally.

Prayer For The Day:

Let me not be concerned with the praise of men,
but may my talent be completely yielded to You, Lord Jesus.

•JULY 25•

> *"How I need your help, especially in my own home*
> *. . ."*
>
> *Psalm 101:2 (TLB)*

I n the marriage ceremony, after the vows are said, the minister solemnly and reverently remarks, "What God hath joined together let no man put asunder." Is not God the third part in a marriage? Should He not be taken into account in the marriage, and in the home that emerges from that marriage? If God joins the couple together at the outset, should not His presence be recognized in the home continually? Many homes are on the rocks today because God has been left out of the domestic picture. With the clash of personalities in a domestic pattern, there must be an integrating force, and the living God is that Force! Many couples think that if they have a better home, get a better job, or live in a different neighborhood, their domestic life will be happier. No! The secret of domestic happiness is to let God, the party of the third part in the marriage contract, have His rightful place in the home. Make peace with Him, and then you can be a real peacemaker in the home.

Prayer For The Day:

In my relationships with those I love, help me to be a peacemaker, Lord. May I always look to You, the Prince of Peace.

•JULY 26•

". . . willing rather to be absent from the body, and to be present with the Lord."
2 Corinthians 5:8

A little boy was riding alone on a train on a hot day when the travelers were extremely uncomfortable; and the scenery was not too interesting as they passed through the desert of Arizona. A lady sitting beside the boy asked him, "Are you tired of the long ride?" The little boy smiled and said, "I'm a little tired, but I don't mind it much. You see, my father is going to meet me when I get to Los Angeles." Sometimes we get a little tired of the burdens of life, but it is exhilarating to know that Jesus Christ will meet us at the end of life's journey. The joy of being with Him forever is beyond the ability of any writer to describe.

Prayer For The Day:

To think You will be waiting for me at the end of this earthly journey! I am filled with unspeakable joy, Lord Jesus.

·JULY 27·

*"Grace be with all them that
love our Lord Jesus Christ in sincerity."*
Ephesians 6:24

Certain relationships in life require from the parties involved
only moderate degrees of devotion. A certain degree of reserve and distance seems to be suitable in such relations as these.
But there are other relationships in life where all this is changed
when friendship becomes love. Two hearts give themselves to each
other to be no longer two, but one. Instead of being separated, their
interest and paths are now together. The reserve and the distance
suitable to mere friendships is fatal in real love. Love gives all and
must have all in return. The wishes of the other party become binding obligations; and the deepest desire of each heart is to know
every secret wish and longing of the other, in order that it may do
all in its power to gratify those desires. Is that the kind of love,
affection, and obedience you have for Christ?

Prayer For The Day:

*Jesus, I say I love You and
yet so often it is a selfish, "taking" love.
Let me love You in such a way that Your desires will be mine.*

·JULY 28·

*". . . make known to the sons
of men his mighty acts, and the glorious
majesty of his kingdom."*
Psalm 145:12

Some years ago I heard about a clergyman who had a friend
who was an actor. The actor was drawing large crowds of
people, and the clergyman was preaching to few in the church. He
said to his actor friend, "Why is it that you draw great crowds, and
I have no audience at all? Your words are sheer fiction, and mine
are unchangeable truth." The actor's reply was quite simple. "I
present my fiction as though it were truth; you present your truth
as though it were fiction." I fear that so often we Christians give the
idea that the truth is fiction by the way we live and by the lack of
dedication to the teachings of our Lord.

Prayer For The Day:

*Lord Jesus, I would completely
yield my life to You, so that others
may know that the Savior I love and serve is the truth!*

·JULY 29·

*"You can never please God without faith,
without depending on him. Anyone who wants
to come to God must believe that
there is a God and that he rewards
those who sincerely look for him."*
Hebrews 11:6 (TLB)

F aith pleases God more than anything else. The Christian life is dependent upon faith. We stand on faith; we live on faith. Faith is loved and honored by God more than any other single thing. The Bible teaches that faith is the only approach that we have to God. No man has sins forgiven, no man goes to heaven, no man has assurance of peace and happiness, until he has faith in Jesus Christ. You may be saying, "God, I believe you are a great person, but I do not believe your Word; I do not believe what you say." In order to please God, you must believe Him. Perhaps your faith is small and weak. It does not matter how big your faith is, but rather, where your faith is. Is it in Christ, the Son of God, who died on the cross for your sins?

Prayer For The Day:

*Lord Jesus, may my faith in You and
Your abundant promises be ever increasing each day.*

·JULY 30·

"Keep thyself pure."
1 Timothy 5:22

S omeone has said, "You cannot help the first look, but the second is sin." Jesus indicated that you can engage in immorality by a *look*. The Bible places the "lust of the eye" right along with other major sins. Listen: "For all that is in the world, the lust of the flesh, and the lust of the eyes, and the pride of life, is not of the

Father, but is of the world." Peter spoke of having "eyes full of adultery." No wonder Job said, "I have made a covenant with my eyes; why then should I think upon a maid?" Your eyes see only what your soul allows them to see.

Prayer For The Day:

May my eyes be on You, Lord Jesus,
for I need Your purity and love to fill my heart and mind.

·JULY 31·

"When we suffer and die
for Christ it only means that we will
begin living with him in heaven."
2 Timothy 2:11 (TLB)

I have a friend who during the depression lost his job, a fortune, a wife, and a home. But he tenaciously held to his faith—the only thing he had left. One day he stopped to watch some men doing stonework on a huge church. One of them was chiseling a triangular piece of stone. "What are you going to do with that?" asked my friend. The workman said, "See that little opening away up there near the spire? Well, I'm shaping this down here, so it will fit in up there." Tears filled the eyes of my friend as he walked away, for it seemed that God had spoken through the workman to explain his ordeal through which he was passing, "I'm shaping you down here, so you'll fit in up there."

Prayer For The Day:

Thank You, Lord, for all the "shaping"
in my life, which brings me closer to You.

·AUGUST 1·

"Pride goes before
destruction, and haughtiness before a fall."
Proverbs 16:18 (TLB)

David, king of ancient Israel, found himself in the midst of a confused national situation. His kingdom was torn by internal strife. Slave hated master; master hated slave. People blamed the government, and government blamed the people. David looked about him and saw that every man thought himself perfect. Each individual placed blame upon other individuals. David knew that if sinful pride continued to increase, his nation would collapse spiritually. He knew that economic depression, moral disintegration, or military defeat inevitably follow spiritual decline. So David turned to God, and it was revealed to him by the Spirit of God that the spiritual tide of his nation could rise no higher than the spiritual level of his own heart. So he fell on his knees in utter humility and prayed, "Search me, O God, and know my heart; try me, and know my thoughts: and see if there by any wicked way in me, and lead me in the way everlasting" (Psalm 139:23,24).

Prayer For The Day:

> *Lord, deliver me from the*
> *sin of pride, and fill me with continuing*
> *humility as I go about the tasks before me this day.*

·AUGUST 2·

> *"And the Lord shall*
> *guide thee continually, and satisfy*
> *thy soul in drought . . ."*
>
> Isaiah 58:11

The soul demands as much attention as the body. It demands fellowship and communion with God. It demands worship, quietness, and meditation. Unless the soul is fed and exercised daily, it becomes weak and shriveled. It remains discontented, confused, restless. Many people turn to alcohol to try to drown the cryings and longings of the soul. Some turn to a new sex experience. Others attempt to quiet the longings of their souls in other ways. Nothing but God ever completely satisfies, because the soul is made for God, and without God it is restless and in secret torment. The first step to God is a realization of your spiritual poverty. The poor in spirit do not measure the worth of life in earthly possessions, which fade away, but in terms of eternal realities, which endure forever. Wise is the man who openly confesses his lack of spiritual wealth and in humility of heart cries, "God, be merciful unto me, a sinner."

Prayer For The Day:

> *As I look to You, my Lord and*
> *my Redeemer, the strivings of my soul*
> *will be satisfied. You alone bring lasting joy.*

·AUGUST 3·

*"There is a way which seemeth
right unto a man, but the end thereof
are the ways of death."*

Proverbs 14:12

A line of human thought that seems right to many people is the idea of self-redemption. Man thinks he must work at righteousness to save himself. After all, it was man who sinned and as we say, "God helps those who help themselves." But a greater truth than this emerges from the Bible—the truth that God helps those who cannot help themselves. We cannot save ourselves. It is noble to be upright if we can. It is admirable to be honest, kind, and compassionate. It would seem that these characteristics would be sufficient to save our souls. But the Bible says that though this way seems right, it is wrong.

Prayer For The Day:

*Father, I know that my attempts at living a
good life are nothing compared to my beloved Savior, Jesus Christ;
but because of Him I can come to You, knowing He has redeemed
me.*

·AUGUST 4·

"You cannot serve two masters: God and money."

Matthew 6:24 (TLB)

Tell me what you think about money, and I will tell you what you think about God, for these two are closely related. A man's heart is closer to his wallet than anything else. It is a staggering fact that for the past few years people have spent ten times as much for luxuries and non-essentials as they have for all charitable and religious purposes. This is a commentary on our shallow and superficial religious faith. While the Bible warns us against greed and selfishness, it does encourage frugality and thrift. Even Jesus said to His disciples after He fed the multitude, "Gather up the fragments that remain, that nothing be lost." Although our Lord had the power to create, He Himself lived frugally and without luxury. John Wesley had a threefold philosophy about money. He said, "Make all you can; keep all you can; and give all you can."

Most of us get all we can, spend all we can; borrow all we can; and give meagerly to God.

Prayer For The Day:

Lord, give me a generous heart
so that others may know Your love and compassion.

✦AUGUST 5✦

"But if we are living in the light of
God's presence, just as Christ does, then
we have wonderful fellowship and joy
with each other, and the blood of Jesus
his Son cleanses us from every sin."
                    1 John 1:7 (TLB)

I received a letter from a man in Charlotte, North Carolina. He said that, until our Charlotte Crusade, he was filled with hatred, bitterness, and prejudice toward people of another race. He had joined one of the extremist organizations and was on the verge of engaging in violence. Out of curiosity he came to the meetings, and one night he was gloriously converted. He said, "All bitterness, hatred, malice, and prejudice immediately left me. I found myself in the counseling room sitting beside a person of another race. Through my tears I gripped the hand of this man, whom a few hours before I would have detested. My racial problem has been solved. I now find that I love all men regardless of the color of their skin." Only Christ can solve the complicated racial problem that is facing the world today. Until people of all races come to accept Christ as Savior, they do not have the ability to love each other. Christ can give supernatural love, which enables you to love even those whom you otherwise could not love.

Prayer For The Day:

Heavenly Father, fill me with that supernatural
love of Jesus that enables me to reach out to the
myriads of people who, in and of myself, would be impossible to
love.

•AUGUST 6•

"Set thy house in order . . ."

2 Kings 20:1

Man condemns himself by his refusal of God's way of salvation. In love and mercy, God is offering to men and women a way of escape, a way of salvation, a hope and anticipation of better things. Man in his blindness, stupidity, stubbornness, egotism, and love of sinful pleasure, refuses God's simple method of escaping the pangs of eternal banishment. Suppose you were sick and called a doctor who came and gave you a prescription. But after thinking it over you decided to ignore his advice and to refuse the medicine. When he returned a few days later, he might have found your condition much worse. Could you blame the doctor? Could you hold him responsible? He gave you the prescription, he prescribed the remedy. But you refused it! Just so, God prescribes the remedy for the ills of the human race. That remedy is personal faith in, and commitment to, Jesus Christ. The remedy is to be "born again." If we deliberately refuse it, then we must suffer the consequence; and we cannot blame God. Is it God's fault that we refuse the remedy?

Prayer For The Day:

Lord Jesus, as You sat looking over Jerusalem, You wept. Give me the same compassion for those who have not accepted Your remedy and been born again.

•AUGUST 7•

"For God hath not given us the spirit of fear; but of power, and of love, and of a sound mind."

2 Timothy 1:7

Many diseases of both the body and mind are self-inflicted. For example, ulcers are often caused by worry and anxiety. Heart attacks are caused many times by overexertion. Unjustified worry, fear, prejudice, hatred, and envy can contribute to mental stress, which could lead to mental illness. So one way to have a healthy mind is to avoid those practices. But the Bible-way to a healthy mind is this, "Let this mind be in you, which was also in

Christ Jesus." If you have the mind of Christ, worry will be offset by trust, enmity by love, and fear by faith.

Prayer For The Day:

> *Fears sometimes seem as if they would*
> *overwhelm me, Lord Jesus, but then I remember Your gift*
> *of power, love, and a healthy mind. Thank You for the promise*
> *of healing and love, as I keep my mind on You, my beloved Lord.*

·AUGUST 8·

> *". . . holy men of God spake as*
> *they were moved by the Holy Spirit."*
> *2 Peter 1:21*

Although one can derive inspiration from any portion of the Scripture, it is better to have an understanding of the general structure of the Bible to get the most out of it. The Old Testament is an account of a nation, Israel. Out of that nation came Jesus Christ, the Savior of the world. The New Testament is an account of a Man, the Son of man, the Savior. God Himself became a man, so that we might know what He is like. His appearance on the earth was the central, most important event of history. The Old Testament gives the background for this event; the New Testament tells the story of its fulfillment. You will find a unity of thought and purpose which indicates that one mind inspired the writing of the whole.

Prayer For The Day:

> *Inspire me, Lord God, as I read the Bible so that I*
> *may be able to understand more clearly Your divine teachings.*

·AUGUST 9·

> *"And all who trust him—God's Son—*
> *to save them have eternal life . . ."*
> *John 3:36 (TLB)*

Currently, Christianity is being compared with other religions as never before. Some so-called Christian leaders even advocate the working out of a system of morals, ethics, and religion that would bring together all the religions of the world. It cannot be done. Jesus Christ is unique. Why insist on the uniqueness of Christ? What did Christ bring into the world that had not appeared before? The Christian answer is that He is the supreme manifestation of God. "God was in Christ, reconciling the world unto himself" (2 Corinthians 5:19). This is the eternal fact of our Christian faith.

Prayer For The Day:

*Beliefs come and go, Lord Jesus, but
You remain—unchanging—for You are the Son of God!*

·AUGUST 10·

*"Eye hath not seen, nor ear heard,
neither have entered into the heart of man,
the things which God hath prepared
for them that love him."*

1 Corinthians 2:9

At the close of the Bible we encounter these words, "And I saw a new heaven and a new earth; for the first heaven and the first earth were passed away." A new world is coming! Each time we pray in the Lord's Prayer, "Thy kingdom come," we should remember that that prayer will be answered. Heaven is described as a new creation in which we shall move in new bodies, possessed of new names, singing new songs, living in a new city government, by a new form of government, and challenged by new prospects of eternity with social justice for all. The paradise that man lost will be regained, but it will be much more. It will not be the old one repaired, patched up, and made over. When God says, "Behold, I make all things new," the emphasis is on *all* things. One day we shall live in a brand-new world. Centuries ago the apostles greeted each other with the word, "Maranatha"—the Lord is coming.

Prayer For The Day:

*Use me, Savior, to hasten Maranatha, as I tell
others that they, too, can be made new through Your divine love.*

·AUGUST 11·

"For by grace are ye saved . . ."
Ephesians 2:8

"Grace," according to the dictionary, is the unmerited favor of God toward mankind. The world "grace" is used over 170 times in the New Testament alone. Grace is not bought. It is a free gift of almighty God to needy mankind. When I picture Jesus Christ dying on the cross, I see the free gift of God's grace in Christ reconciling the world unto Himself. I sing with the songwriter, "Amazing grace, how sweet the sound that saved a wretch like me. I once was lost, but now am found, was blind, but now I see." Your human mind, with its philosophy of an equal return for favors done, can hardly comprehend the full meaning of this grace of God. But when you catch, by the inspiration of God, its full meaning, you will leave the limits of human reasoning and revel in the spiritual riches of divine truth and privilege. Yes, the grace of God is a reality. Thousands have tried, tested, and proved that it is more than a cold creed, a docile doctrine, or a tedious theory. The grace of God has been tested in the crucible of human experience, and has been found to be more than an equal for the problems and sins of humanity.

Prayer For The Day:

Lord, this day help me to come to a more full and abundant awareness of Your bountiful grace. Stimulate me to serve You.

·AUGUST 12·

"For my people [are]
foolish, they have not known me . . ."
Jeremiah 4:22

No man is more pathetic than he who is in great need and is not aware of it. Remember Samson? Standing there in the valley of Sorek, surrounded by the lords of the Philistines, ". . . he wist not that the Lord was departed from him." It has been truly said, "No man is so ignorant as he who knows nothing and knows not that he knows nothing. No man is so sick as he who has a fatal disease and is not aware of it. No man is so poor as he who is destitute, and yet thinks he is rich." The pitiable thing about the

Pharisees was not so much their hypocrisy as it was their utter lack of knowledge of how poor they actually were in the sight of God. There is always something pathetic about a man who thinks he is rich when he is actually poor, who thinks he is good when he is actually vile, who thinks he is educated when he is actually illiterate.

Prayer For The Day:

*Might I always remember
the poverty of my soul before Your
love invaded my life, Lord Jesus, and I knew You as Savior.*

•AUGUST 13•

*"Christ died and rose
again . . . so that he can be our Lord both
while we live and when we die."*

Romans 14:9 (TLB)

With a frequency that is amazing, the Bible affirms the fact of the bodily resurrection of Christ. Perhaps the most direct of all its statements is Luke's account in the book of Acts, where he reports, "To whom also he shewed himself alive after his passion by many infallible proofs, being seen of them forty days" (Acts 1:3). What are we going to do with these "many infallible proofs"? Someone asked my colleague George Beverly Shea how much he knew about God. He said, "I don't know much, but what I do know has changed my life." We may not be able to take all of this evidence into a scientific laboratory and prove it; but, if we accept any fact of history, we must accept the fact that Jesus Christ rose from the dead.

Prayer For The Day:

*All the arguments concerning Your existence
are refuted, Lord Jesus, as I feel Your presence each day. It
causes my soul to rejoice knowing You, my living Lord, are with
me!*

· AUGUST 14 ·

"But of him are ye in Christ Jesus,
who of God is made unto us wisdom . . ."
                              1 Corinthians 1:30

I believe we ought to get all the education we can, but we dare not make it our god. John Dewey once defined education as the systematic, purposeful reconstruction of experience; but so much of modern education leaves out God. What we are actually doing is reconstructing our sins. We expand our sins, enlarge them, multiply them. We need education, but not just for the mind and the body; we also need education for the spirit. Man has a spirit, and in our educational system today we need a spiritual emphasis. If we bring up a generation that lacks the wisdom that God can give, they can turn into educated savages and fools. "The fear of the Lord is the beginning of wisdom" and education. Let's make sure our rock is God.

Prayer For The Day:

Almighty God, I am grateful to You
that Your Word educates my spirit and makes me whole.

· AUGUST 15 ·

"These things that were written in the Scriptures
so long ago are to teach us . . ."
                              Romans 15:4 (TLB)

I n the wonders of nature we see God's laws in operation. Who has not looked up at the stars on a cloudless night and marveled in silent awe at the glory of God's handiwork? Who has not felt his heart lifted in the spring of the year, as he sees all creation bursting with new life and vigor? In the beauty and abundance around us we see the magnitude of God's power and the infinite detail of His planning; but nature tells us nothing of God's love or God's grace. Conscience tells us in our innermost being of the presence of God and of the moral difference between good and evil; but this is a fragmentary message, in no way as distinct and comprehensive as the lessons of the Bible. It is only in its pages that we find the clear and unmistakable message upon which all true Christianity is based.

Prayer For The Day:

As I read Your Word, almighty God,
clear my mind of needless thoughts, so
that I may be aware of Your message for me this day.

✦AUGUST 16✦

"I will give to the thirsty the springs
of the Water of Life—as a gift!"
Revelation 21:6 (TLB)

G od says that only those who hunger after righteousness will
receive it. God thrusts this heavenly manna on no one. You
must desire it, above everything else. Your yearning for God must
supersede all other desires. It must be like a gnawing hunger and a
burning thirst.

Prayer For The Day:

Almighty God, my soul is parched
and I'm so hungry without the spiritual food
You so desire to give me. Take away anything in
my life that would cause me not to give You pre-eminence.

✦AUGUST 17✦

Mott's B'day
1909

"Look at the birds! They don't worry
about what to eat—they don't need to sow or
reap or store up food—for your heavenly
Father feeds them. And you are far more
valuable to him than they are."
Matthew 6:26 (TLB)

S ome section hands on a British railroad found a thrush's nest
under a rail. Peacefully sitting on her eggs, the hen was undis-
turbed by the roar of the fast trains above and around her. Someone has written a little verse which goes:

"Said the robin to the sparrow,
'I should really like to know,
Why these anxious human beings
Rush about and worry so.'
Said the sparrow to the robin,
Friend, I think that it must be,

That they have no heavenly Father
Such as cares for you and me.'"

Jesus used the carefree attitude of the birds to underscore the fact that worrying is unnatural. I am learning in my own life, day by day, to keep my mind centered on Christ, and the worries and anxieties and concerns of the world pass, and nothing but "perfect peace" is left in the human heart. God has taken the responsibility for our care and worry.

Prayer For The Day:

Lord Jesus, I'm happiest when I'm fully trusting You. This day help me to be constantly grateful for Your care and faithfulness.

·AUGUST 18·

*"Lay up for yourselves
treasures in heaven . . ."*

Matthew 6:20

Many young people are building their lives on the rock of materialism. I find across the country a deep economic discontent among people in every walk of life. People want more and more things. They forget that we are enjoying the highest standard of living the world has ever known. We still have poverty, and hundreds of agencies are trying to do something about it; but we are dissatisfied. We want more, more, more. But Jesus said, "You cannot serve God and money." He said that a man's life does not consist in the abundance of the things that he possesses. Adolf Berle, in his study of power, points out that riches often make people solitary and lonely and, of course, afraid. Many times a rich man knows loneliness and fear, because when he makes wealth his god, it leaves him empty. You see, without God life loses its zest and purpose and meaning.

Prayer For The Day:

*Knowing You, my heavenly Father,
brings richness to my life and soul.*

•AUGUST 19•

"Let the word of Christ dwell in you richly
in all wisdom; teaching and admonishing one
another in psalms and hymns and spiritual
songs, singing with grace in your
hearts to the Lord."

Colossians 3:16

C hristians are to rejoice. To do that, you need only to think of the great things God has done for you. Then we are told not to be anxious, but in our prayers to make our requests known to God. In your biggest problems you have One to whom you can go; and before Him you can pour out your heart with the assurance that He will not leave you without an answer to that great problem. Then we are to fill our minds with those things that are good. They are mentioned in the Scriptures as being things that are true, honorable, just, pure, lovely, of good report, and of virtue. It is upon these things that we are to think. Live positively, not negatively. Once you learn that secret, God will have given you the victory.

Prayer For The Day:

You know what troubles me today,
Lord Jesus. In faith, I give it all over to
You and now praise You, knowing Your love will not fail.

•AUGUST 20•

"The disciples were filled
with joy, and with the Holy Ghost."

Acts 13:52

T he Bible speaks of three kinds of pleasure. There is lustful pleasure, the lust of the flesh, and Scripture says it is sinful and wrong. There is legitimate pleasure, which is not wrong, but we are not to become so preoccupied with its activities that it takes the place of God. Then there is a third kind of pleasure, lasting pleasure. Do you have that kind? It does not depend on circumstances or feelings. It is the pleasure that runs deep and comes from the Spirit of God.

Prayer For The Day:

Almighty God, may my pleasure always
come from being filled with the joy of Your Holy Spirit.

·AUGUST 21·

"And there shall be no more curse;
but the throne of God and of the Lamb shall be
in it; and his servants shall serve him."
                                        Revelation 22:3

The Bible indicates that heaven will be a place of great under-standing and knowledge of things that we never learned down here. Sir Isaac Newton, when an old man, said to one who praised his wisdom, "I am as a child on the seashore picking up a pebble here and a shell there, but the great ocean of truth still lies before me." And Thomas Edison once said, "I do not know one millionth part of one percent about anything." Many of the mysteries of God—the heartaches, trials, disappointments, tragedies, and the silence of God in the midst of suffering—will be revealed in heaven.

Prayer For The Day:

All the questions will be answered,
loving Father, when I take my place in heaven to praise You.

·AUGUST 22·

"For we know that when this tent we live in
now is taken down—when we die and leave these
bodies—we will have wonderful new
bodies in heaven, homes that will be ours
forevermore, made for us by God himself,
and not by human hands."
                                  2 Corinthians 5:1 (TLB)

Death, to the Christian, is the exchanging of a tent for a build-ing. Here we are as pilgrims or gypsies, living in a frail, flimsy home; subject to disease, pain, and peril. But at death we exchange this crumbling, disintegrating tent for a house not made with hands, eternal in the heavens. The wandering wayfarer comes into his own at death and is given the title to a mansion which will never deteriorate nor crumble. Do you think that God, who has provided so amply for living, has made no provision for dying? The Bible says we are strangers in a foreign land. This world is not our home; our citizenship is in heaven. When a Christian dies, he goes into the presence of Christ. He goes to heaven to spend eternity with God.

·AUGUST 23·

*"Let us search and try
our ways, and turn again to the Lord."*
Lamentations 3:40

Our modern philosophy of self-reliance and self-sufficiency has caused many to believe that we can make the grade without God. "Religion," they argue, "may be all right for certain emotional people, but you can't beat a man who believes in himself." But this self-confident generation has produced more alcoholics, more dope addicts, more criminals, more wars, more broken homes, more assaults, more embezzlements, more murders, and more suicides than any other generation that ever lived. It is time for all of us to take stock of our failures, blunders, and costly mistakes. It is about time that we are putting less confidence in ourselves and more trust and faith in God.

Prayer For The Day:

*As I examine my heart, I see so much of
self there. I ask that You would forgive me,
Lord—my confidence will be in Your leading.*

·AUGUST 24·

*"Overwhelming victory is ours through Christ
who loved us enough to die for us."*
Romans 8:37 (TLB)

The basic problem facing our world is not just social inequity, or lack of education, or even physical hunger. We are finding that highly educated and well-fed people have greeds, hates, passions, and lusts that are not eliminated by education. The root of sin in each of our hearts is extremely deep, and this is the basic cause of the world's problems; only the fire of the Lord can burn it out. This is precisely what Christ came to do. He didn't come to treat symptoms. He came to get at the very heart of man's disease.

Prayer For The Day:

Father, root out the sin in my life—
the shortcomings that are there—and fill me with
Your love, so I may fight against the evil present in the world
today.

·AUGUST 25·

"Whatsoever things are
pure . . . think on these things."
                    Philippians 4:8

Nowhere does the Bible teach that sex in itself is a sin. Man in his sinful nature has taken what was intended to be a glorious and complete act of love between two people and has made it something low, cheap, and dirty. The Bible is one of the world's outspoken books on the subject of sex, and the Bible condemns sex outside the bonds of matrimony. The fact that immorality is rampant throughout the nation doesn't make it right; the fact that some clergymen may condone it doesn't make it right. The Bible says, "There is a way that seemeth right unto a man; but the end thereof are the ways of death" (Proverbs 16:25). Under Jewish law adultery was punishable by death. Under God's law today it also results in spiritual death.

Prayer For The Day:

All around me, breaking Your laws is made
so enticing, Father. Help me to keep my eyes on Jesus.

·AUGUST 26·

"And the disciples
were called Christians . . ."
                    Acts 11:26

In the third century Cyprian, the Bishop of Carthage, wrote to his friend Donatus, "It is a bad world, Donatus, an incredibly bad world. But I have discovered in the midst of it a quiet and holy people, who have learned a great secret. They have found a joy which is a thousand times better than any of the pleasures of our sinful life. They are despised and persecuted, but they care not. They are masters of their souls. They have overcome the world.

These people, Donatus, are Christians . . . and I am one of them."
If you have repented of your sins and have received Christ as Savior, then you, too, are one of them.

Prayer For The Day:

*Today, Lord God, I remember all those Christians who have gone
before me and thank You for the inspiration of their memory.
May I never take for granted the heritage I have in Christ Jesus.*

·AUGUST 27·

*"Just as you used to be slaves
to all kinds of sin, so now you must let
yourselves be slaves to all that is right and holy."*
Romans 6:19 (TLB)

W e have heard the modern expression, "Don't fight it—it's
bigger than both of us." Those who are meek do not fight
back at life. They learn the secret of surrender, or yielding to God.
He then fights for us! Instead of filling your mind with resentments,
abusing your body by sinful diversion, and damaging your soul by
willfulness, humbly give all over to God. Your conflicts will disappear and your inner tensions will vanish into thin air. Then your
life will begin to count for something. You will have the feeling of
belonging to life. Boredom will melt away, and you will become
vibrant with hope and expectation. Because you are meekly
yielded, you will begin to "inherit the earth" of good things, which
God holds in store for all who trust Him with their all.

Prayer For The Day:

*Let me yield to You this day, Father,
all my innermost thoughts. I cannot hide from You.*

·AUGUST 28·

*"Unto every one of us is given grace
according to the measure of the gift of Christ."*
Ephesians 4:7

T he Christian life is never spoken of in the Bible as a bed of
roses. It is uphill, because society is coming one way and the
Christian is going the opposite way. But Jesus said that in the midst

of your problems, in the midst of your difficulties, He will be there to give you grace and peace. Underneath all the troubles, will be the "still waters" that the Great Shepherd can provide. Many people are trying to steady themselves by taking tranquilizers. Jesus is the greatest tranquilizer of all. He can straighten out your life and put you back on center. Let Him take full control. You'll go on your way rejoicing, as did those in the New Testament who met Jesus.

Prayer For The Day:

I need Your calmness and strength, for
there are many trials to face, Lord Jesus. By faith
I reach out to You, and receive the gift of Your peace in my life.

•AUGUST 29•

"You are living a brand-new kind of
life . . . more and more like Christ who created
this new life within you."
Colossians 3:10 (TLB)

A long-haired blond from a Southern university seemed to be enjoying a satisfactory student career when her grades began to slip. "Life had become one long case of the blahs," she confessed later. "I wasn't walking around with a steady load of blues, but I wasn't enjoying life. Small things made me blow up. I met some kids who seemed to know something I didn't know, but I couldn't get in on it. We went to several meetings, and one night the speaker said that we don't earn God's love. He takes us as we are. It was then I realized it wasn't a matter of clocking up a certain number of hours doing good deeds. Instead, I had to make myself available. Through faith, I had to let Him take over. It came together all at once, when I accepted Christ as my personal Savior. I know that God is in me in everything I do. My life has taken on a new dimension." Does your life have this new dimension? It can! Just begin now with Jesus Christ! When you make this beginning, it will be your first step toward realizing personal fulfillment, meaning, and joy.

Prayer For The Day:

By faith, loving Father, I ask
You to take over every part of
my life—draw me closer to Your Son, my Savior, Jesus Christ.

•AUGUST 30•

*"Ye have heard that it hath been said,
Thou shalt love thy neighbor, and hate thine
enemy. But I say unto you, Love your enemies,
bless them that curse you, do good to them
that hate you, and pray for them which
despitefully use you, and persecute you; that
ye may be the children of your Father
which is in heaven . . ."*

Matthew 5:43-45

When H. G. Wells summed up the influence of Jesus in history, he said, "Is it any wonder that this Galilean is too much for our small hearts?" And yet the heart of man, though small, is big enough for Christ to live in, if man will only make room for Him. Christ instilled the spirit of Christian love in His followers, so that they lived without malice and died without rancor. The love that Christ talked about can only be given to us by God. It is one of the fruits of the Spirit. When you come to Jesus Christ, He transforms you. Your past is forgiven. You receive a power to love men, beyond your natural ability to love.

Prayer For The Day:

*Instill in me, dear Father, Your same
Spirit of love which enabled the disciples to live with true charity.*

•AUGUST 31•

"The righteous hath hope in his death."

Proverbs 14:32

We don't like to talk about death; it's the forbidden subject of our generation. Yet it's real for all of us. Sometimes on television I see motion pictures featuring actors who are no longer living. They seem very much alive in the picture, but they are dead. Some of them were my personal friends. Death is real, and when we die, that is a battle we have to fight all alone. Nobody can be with us in that hour, but David said he had found an answer that would take the fear of death away. David said that there is an answer to death, there is a hope beyond death. That hope is centered in the risen Christ. Paul wrote that to be "absent from the body" is to be "present with the Lord." So the fear of death is removed.

Prayer For The Day:

*Lord Jesus, with complete trust I look
toward that day when my soul will be with You for eternity.*

•SEPTEMBER 1•

*"Follow me, and I will
make you fishers of men."*
Matthew 4:19

Jesus Himself was the first missionary! He did not sit by passively and let those who happened to be interested in His teaching come to Him. He went out where the sick, the sorrowing, and the sad were, and expounded His message of joy, healing, and salvation. Even at a tender age, He went to the Temple and "taught" the doctors and lawyers who were entrenched in the old traditions. He found His way to the seaside and intruded upon the life of the commonest of laborers, saying, "Follow me, and I will make you fishers of men." Wherever He went He challenged, uprooted, and changed men. And at length they nailed Him to a cross because He had upset their selfish, secure, smug way of life. Not only was Jesus a missionary, but He pledged His followers to be missionaries, too!

Prayer For The Day:

*Wherever I go, it is a mission field
for You, Lord. Help me to be conscious
of this, so that I may tell others the joyous message.*

•SEPTEMBER 2•

*"For we wrestle not against flesh and blood,
but against principalities, against powers,
against the rulers of the darkness of this world,
against spiritual wickedness in high places."*
Ephesians 6:12

All life is a struggle—that is the nature of things. Even within our physical bodies, doctors tell us, a conflict for supremacy is going on. The bacteria in our bloodstream are waging a constant war against alien germs. The red corpuscles fight the white corpuscles constantly in an effort to maintain life within the body. A battle is also raging in the spiritual realm. "We fight," the Bible says, "against the rulers of the darkness of this world." Darkness hates light. I have a dog that would rather dig up a moldy carcass to chew on than to have the finest, cleanest meal. He can't help it— that is his nature. Men cannot help that it is their nature to respond to the lewd, the salacious, and the vile. They will have difficulty doing otherwise until they are born again. And until they are changed by the power of Christ, they will likely be at enmity against those who are associated with Christ.

Prayer For The Day:

The battles of life must be faced, but
I know they will not be faced without You, my heavenly Father.

◆SEPTEMBER 3◆

"Even while we were still there
with you we gave you this rule: 'He who
does not work shall not eat.'"
2 Thessalonians 3:10 (TLB)

One of the Christian's responsibilities in following Christ is to have a new attitude toward work. So many young people want Christ without responsibility. Jesus was not a drop-out. As a carpenter, He worked hard with His hands. The Apostle Paul made tents for a living while he carried on the work that God assigned him. Whatever work a Christian does is done unto the Lord. He should do his best at whatever his trade or vocation. He should be faithful, clean, and honest.

Prayer For The Day:

Thank You for teaching us
that work is a blessing, Lord Jesus.

◆SEPTEMBER 4◆

"Who his own self bare our
sins in his own body on the tree . . ."
1 Peter 2:24

Jesus worked all His life. But the greatest work that Jesus did was not in the carpenter's shop, nor even at the marriage feast of Cana where He turned the water into wine. The greatest work that

Jesus did was not when He made the blind to see, the deaf to hear, the dumb to speak, nor even the dead to rise. The greatest work that Jesus did was not when He taught as One having authority, or when He scathingly denounced the Pharisees for their hypocrisy. The greatest work that Jesus did was not in the great ethical program He presented to mankind—that program which has become the foundation for Western culture. What, then, was His greatest work? His greatest work was achieved in those three dark hours on Calvary. Christ's greatest work was His dying for us.

Prayer For The Day:

*When I consider the work of Jesus
on this earth—which led to His supreme sacrifice—
I pray all my labor this day will glorify You, my beloved Savior.*

·SEPTEMBER 5·

*"Come unto me,
all ye that labor . . ."*

Matthew 11:28

J esus had a great deal to say about labor. He knew that a laboring man needs rest and recreation. We Americans have Labor Day—a day in which the wheels of industry stop and the entire nation is reminded of the tremendous contribution that labor has made to the American way of life. Jesus Himself was a laboring man. In His biography we are told that He was a carpenter. Wouldn't you like to have been able to spend a day in Joseph's little shop and to watch Jesus use the hammer and saw? Sometimes we forget that Jesus was human as well as divine. He had calluses on His hands. If the chisel had slipped and cut His fingers, His blood would have been red and warm like ours. He knew what it meant to work long hours, to come in at night tired and weary.

Prayer For The Day:

*Remembering Your labor here on earth
helps me to realize that all work is sacred
if done as unto You, Lord Jesus. Help me to rest
so that, refreshed, I may seek to please You in everything I do.*

·SEPTEMBER 6·

*"Clothe yourself
with this new nature."*

Ephesians 4:24 (TLB)

I n Texas they tell a story about a man who used to hitch his horse every morning in front of the saloon. One morning the saloon-keeper came out and found that the horse was hitched in front of the Methodist church. He saw the man walking down the street and called out, "Say, why is your horse hitched in front of the Methodist church this morning?" The man turned around and said, "Well, last night I was converted in the revival meeting, and I've changed hitching posts." That's what it means to be born again. That's what it means to be converted. It means that you changed hitching posts.

Prayer For The Day:

*May I live in such a way that people
will know that I am bound in the freedom of Your love.*

·SEPTEMBER 7·

*"I will dwell in the
house of the Lord for ever."*

Psalm 23:6

W hat will heaven be like? Just as there is a mystery to hell, so there is a mystery to heaven. Yet I believe the Bible teaches that heaven is a literal place. Is it one of the stars? I don't know, I can't even speculate. The Bible doesn't inform us. I believe that out there in space where there are one thousand million galaxies, each a hundred thousand light years or more in diameter, God can find some place to put us in heaven. I'm not worried about where it is. I know it will be where Jesus is. Christians don't have to go around discouraged and despondent, with their shoulders bent. Think of it—the joy, the peace, the sense of forgiveness that He gives you, and then heaven, too.

Prayer For The Day:

*Whatever I face, Lord, my heart rejoices
in the knowledge of my ultimate destination—
heaven—where I will live with You for eternity!*

M's B'day
1989

•SEPTEMBER 8•

"God loveth a cheerful giver."
2 Corinthians 9:7

T he greatest blessing of giving is not on the financial side of the ledger but on the spiritual side. You receive a sense of being honest with God. You receive a consciousness that you are in partnership with God—that you are doing something constructive— that you are working with Him to reach the world for Jesus Christ. You are also enabled to hold on to this world's goods loosely because the eternal values are always in view. How do you give? Is it liberally and cheerfully? Or is it sparingly and grudgingly? If you have been giving God the leftovers of your substance and your life, you have been missing the true joy and blessing of Christian giving and living.

Prayer For The Day:

*Forgive me, almighty God, for so often giving
You the leftovers. In my heart I know I can never outgive You.*

C's B'day
1940

•SEPTEMBER 9•

*"He . . . has given you
a full understanding of the truth."*
1 Corinthians 1:5 (TLB)

T here is never any conflict between true science and our Christian faith. It is my own feeling that when all of the truth is known, it will be found that the Genesis story is a wonderfully accurate record of what took place when the world was created. This may be a telescoped record, giving only major points, but I believe it is scientifically accurate. To discard the Bible because we do not understand everything in it, or in the world, would be a foolish thing to do. Let me also suggest that teachers should confine themselves to those areas in which they are qualified. I have known unbelievers to attack the Christian faith through their teaching, even when they did not have the remotest idea of what true Christianity is. For instance, one does not send an art critic to write up a football game, or a sports writer to evaluate a painting. Ask God to give you the wisdom to keep things in their proper perspective, and—above all—faithfully read your Bible and pray every day. If you do, God will give you the faith and wisdom you need to meet any problem.

Prayer For The Day:

*Father, each day as I read the Bible You reveal to me
more of the reality of Your love and wisdom. I delight in Your
Word!*

•SEPTEMBER 10•

"Be thou faithful unto death . . ."
Revelation 2:10

I n our day much of the world believes little or nothing. People
are broad but shallow. Agnosticism, anxiety, emptiness, mean-
inglessness, have gripped much of the world—and even the church.
Our youth are desperately searching for a purpose and a meaning
in their lives. They are searching for fulfillment which they are not
finding in sex and drugs. By contrast, our Pilgrim forebears stand
as shining examples of men who were narrow but deep, certain of
what they believed, unswerving in their loyalty, and passionately
dedicated to the God they trusted, and for whom they would will-
ingly have died. I say to you, more than 350 years after the Pilgrim
Fathers landed in the New World: Dream great dreams, embrace
great principles, renew your hope, but above all, like them, believe
in the Christ who alone can give total meaning and an ultimate goal
to your life. "For in Him we live and move and have our being."

Prayer For The Day:

*May I always be faithful to
my belief in You, Lord Jesus Christ.
Where there is despair, use me to bring Your hope.*

•SEPTEMBER 11•

Mom died today in 1971

The WTC was destroyed today by terrorists in 2001

*"God . . . is the one who
invited you into this wonderful friendship with
his Son, even Christ our Lord."*
1 Corinthians 1:9 (TLB)

T he question remains, "How can God be just—that is, true to
Himself in nature and true to Himself in holiness—and yet
justify the sinner?" Because each man had to bear his own sins, all
mankind was excluded from helping, since each was contaminated

with the same disease. The only solution was for an innocent party to volunteer to die physically and spiritually as a substitution before God. This innocent party would have to take man's judgment, penalty, and death. But where was such an individual? Certainly, there was none on earth. There was only one possibility. God's own Son was the only personality in the universe who had the capacity to bear in His own body the sins of the world. Only God's Son was infinite and thus able to die for all.

Prayer For The Day:

Lord Jesus, Lamb of God,
in adoration I thank You for the love that
made You willing to suffer and die on the cross for my sin.

•SEPTEMBER 12•

"Blessed are the meek;
for they shall inherit the earth."
                              Matthew 5:5

In His characteristic way Jesus was saying something quite shocking and revolutionary to His listener with these words, "Happy are the meek." He was saying something quite the opposite of our modern concept of the way to happiness. We say, "Happy are the clever, for they shall inherit the admiration of their friends"; "Happy are the aggressive, for they shall inherit a career"; "Happy are the rich, for they shall inherit a world of friends and a house full of modern gadgets." Jesus did not say, "Be meek and you shall inherit the earth." He, more than anyone else, knew that meekness was a gift of God, a result of rebirth. Jesus was not issuing a command in this Beatitude nor saying, "You ought to be meek, that is the way to live." No! He was saying that if we want to find the secret of happiness, that if we want to enjoy living, then "meekness" is a basic key.

Prayer For The Day:

May I truly reflect Your meekness in my life, Lord.

•SEPTEMBER 13•

Everything else is worthless
when compared with the priceless gain
of knowing Christ Jesus . . ."

Philippians 3:8 (TLB)

"**W**here is Jesus Christ?" Innumerable students are studying Him and deciding whether or not Christ and the Gospel really matter—whether He is relevant in this modern age. C.S. Lewis, a professor of Medieval and Renaissance Literature at Oxford and later at Cambridge, had to do the same thing. He spent his life exploring the great literature of centuries. In his remarkable autobiography, *Surprised by Joy*, he tells of his pilgrimage from atheism to Christianity. His turning point came with the realization that the writing with the deepest meaning and greatest content was based on a deep, personal faith in God, by men like Augustine, Blaise Pascal, George Macdonald.

Prayer For The Day:

There is nothing more I desire, Lord Jesus,
than to walk closely with You—my Savior and Lord.

•SEPTEMBER 14•

"By this shall all men know
that ye are my disciples, if ye have
love one to another."

John 13:35

The human soul is a lonely thing. It must have the assurance of companionship. Left entirely to itself, it cannot enjoy anything. God said in the beginning, "It is not good that man should dwell alone" (Genesis 2:18). The creation of Eve was the beginning of human companionship. God's people are a body, not intended to function separately, not intended to be unconcerned for one another. The only true body in the world is the Church. The world may talk grandly of brotherhood, but in reality its philosophy is "each man for himself." God's children are guaranteed the richest and truest friendship, both here and hereafter. Only in a true friendship and a true love do we find a genuine basis for peace. Only God can break down the national and racial barriers that divide men today. Only God can supply that love that we must have for our fellowman. We will never build brotherhood of man upon earth until we are believers in Christ Jesus. The only true cohesive power in the world is Christ. He alone can bind human hearts together in genuine love.

Prayer For The Day:

>*Father, teach me true brotherhood in Jesus Christ.*

·SEPTEMBER 15·

>*"And how does a man benefit if he*
>*gains the whole world and loses his soul*
>*in the process? For is anything*
>*worth more than his soul?"*
>
>Mark 8:36,37 (TLB)

In the world in which we live, we give most attention to satisfying the appetites of the body and practically none to the soul. Consequently, we are one-sided. We become fat physically and materially, while spiritually we are lean, weak, and anemic. The soul actually demands as much attention as the body. It demands fellowship and communion with God. It demands worship, quietness, and meditation. Unless the soul is fed and exercised daily, it becomes weak and shriveled. It remains discontented, confused, restless. Many people turn to alcohol to try to drown the cryings and longings of the soul. Some turn to a new sex experience. Others attempt to quiet the longings of their souls in other ways. But nothing but God ever completely satisfies, because the soul was made for God, and without God it is restless and in secret torment.

Prayer For The Day:

>*Dear Lord, I thank You that*
>*when my soul cried out for forgiveness and love,*
>*You were there. Today help me to live as Your child should.*

•SEPTEMBER 16•

"We preach Christ crucified . . ."
1 Corinthians 1:23

One of the great needs in the church today is for every Christian to become enthusiastic about his faith in Jesus Christ. This is the essence of vital spiritual experience. The apostles had been with Christ, and they could not help but testify to that which they had seen and heard. Every Christian should become an ambassador of Christ with the splendid abandon of Francis of Assisi. Every Christian should be so intoxicated with Christ and so filled with holy fervor that nothing could ever quench his ardor. The Gospel that Paul preached seemed madness to the world of his day. Let us have this madness! Let us capture some of the magnificent obsession that these early Christians had! Let us go forth as men and women filled with the Spirit of God!

Prayer For The Day:

Create in me, Lord, the abandonment
to reach out unreservedly with the message of Your love.

•SEPTEMBER 17•

"The tongue is a small thing
but what enormous damage it can do . . ."
James 3:5 (TLB)

There is a story of a woman in England who came to her vicar with a troubled conscience. The vicar knew her to be an habitual gossip—she had maligned nearly everyone in the village. "How can I make amends?" she pleaded. The vicar said. "If you want to make peace with your conscience, take a bag of goose feathers and drop one on the porch of each one you have slandered." When she had done so, she came back to the vicar and said, "Is that all?" "No," said the wise old minister, "you must go now and gather up every feather and bring them all back to me." After a long time the woman returned without a single feather. "The wind has blown them all away," she said. "My good woman," said the vicar, "so it is with gossip. Unkind words are easily dropped, but we can never take them back again."

Prayer For The Day:

> *Might my words about another be ones that*
> *are spoken in the spirit of Your loving kindness, Father.*

•SEPTEMBER 18•

> *"For here have we no continuing city, but*
> *we seek one to come."*
>
> *Hebrews 13:14*

One of the basic desires of the soul is to live on and on. Self-preservation is the first law of nature. People may grow tired of aches and pains and the decrepitude of old age, but they do not grow tired of life itself. God has arranged to satisfy this yearning of the soul to live forever, and the desire to be free from pain and sickness and trouble. People are little creatures with big capacities, finite beings with infinite desires, deserving nothing but demanding all. God made people with this huge capacity and desire in order that He might come in and completely satisfy that desire. God made the human heart so big that only He can fill it. He made it demand so much that only He can supply that demand . . . Jesus Christ is the only one who holds the keys of death. In His death and resurrection He took the sting out of death, and now God offers eternal life to every person who puts his trust and faith in His Son Jesus Christ.

Prayer For The Day:

> *Lord Jesus, when I come*
> *to the end of this earthly life, You will be*
> *there to guide me to my heavenly home. Thank You, my loving*
> *Father.*

•SEPTEMBER 19•

> *"Every one of us shall*
> *give account of himself to God."*
>
> *Romans 14:12*

I do not quarrel with Karl Marx's statement that "religion is the opiate of the people." I never try to defend religion. Religion has spawned wars. Many so-called religious people have been characterized by prejudice, pride, bickering, and even tolerance for slavery. However, I would call you to a simple faith in Jesus, who said, "Love your neighbor as yourself." Are you really concerned? Are you disappointed with society? If you are, I challenge you to take the first step. I challenge you to look at yourself.

Prayer For The Day:

Forgive me, for so often failing
to love my neighbor. May my
life speak to others of Your love and compassion, Lord Jesus
Christ.

·SEPTEMBER 20·

"It is God himself who has made us what
we are and given us new lives from Christ Jesus;
and long ages ago he planned that we should
spend these lives in helping others."
Ephesians 2:10 (TLB)

Happiness and all of the unlimited benefits which flow from the storehouse of heaven are contingent upon our relationship to God. Absolute dependency and absolute yieldedness are the conditions of being His child. Only His children are entitled to receive those things that lend themselves to happiness; and in order to be His child, there must be the surrender of the will to Him. We must admit we are poor before we can be made rich. We must admit we are destitute before we can become children of adoption. When we realize that all our own goodness is as filthy rags in God's sight, and become aware of the destructive power of our stubborn wills; when we realize our absolute dependence upon the grace of God through faith and nothing more, then we have started on the road to happiness. Man does not come to know God through works—he comes to know God by faith through grace. You cannot work your way toward happiness and heaven, you cannot moralize your way, you cannot reform your way, you cannot buy your way. It comes as a gift of God through Christ.

Prayer For The Day:

Ever impress upon us, Lord Jesus,
that it is through grace that we came to know
You; that it is because of You that we stand righteous before You.

• SEPTEMBER 21 •

*"Since earliest times men have seen
the earth and sky and all God made, and have
known of his existence and
great eternal power . . ."*

Romans 1:20 (TLB)

I f you try to rationalize God exhaustively, you will fail. There
are mysteries about God that we will never understand in this
life. How can the small and finite, limited to time and space, understand an infinite God! We should not think it strange that it is impossible to explain many mysteries in the realm of matter. Who can
explain why objects are always attracted to the center of the earth?
Who can fathom the law of gravity? Newton discovered it, but he
could not explain it. Who can explain the miracle of reproduction?
. . . Thus many evidences and many arguments could be advanced
to indicate there is a God. Yet the plain truth is this: God cannot be
proved by mere rationalization. He cannot be contained in a tiny
man-made test tube or confined to an algebraic formula. If God can
be fully proved by the human mind, then He is no greater than the
mind that proves Him.

Prayer For The Day:

*Lord God almighty, although my finite
mind cannot comprehend the magnitude of Your greatness,
I have felt Your presence in the quiet of my heart and I am
gladdened.*

• SEPTEMBER 22 •

*"There is salvation in no one else! Under all heaven
there is no other name for men to call upon to save
them."*

Acts 4:12 (TLB)

S alvation is an act of God. It is initiated by God, wrought by
God, and sustained by God. The faith that saves the soul is
described as faith in Christ as the Son of God—not as a good man
or a great man, but as the uniquely begotten Son of the living God!
This is consistent with the witness of the entire New Testament and
with the proclamations of the first preachers of the Gospel. All
proclaim the necessity of faith in Jesus Christ as deity.

· SEPTEMBER 23 ·

*". . . who will not suffer you
to be tempted above that ye are able . . ."*
1 Corinthians 10:13

I t is Satan's purpose to steal the seed of truth from your heart by sending distracting thoughts. It should encourage you to know that the devil considers you a good enough Christian to use as a target. The difference between a Christian and a non-Christian is: though they both may have good and evil thoughts, Christ gives His followers strength to select the right rather than the wrong. You see a man going to prayer meeting with a Bible under his arm. That man was undoubtedly tempted to stay at home, go bowling, or to some other activity. But, as these diverse thoughts came to his mind, he made the right selection, and headed for the church. Another man walks through the night to a bar. It no doubt occurred to him that he had best stay home with his family. But he yielded to the negative thought, and gave in to his lower appetites. It is not the temptations you have, but the decision you make about them that counts.

Prayer For The Day:

*Decisions will have to be made each day, Lord.
With Your strength and wisdom, help me to make the right ones.*

· SEPTEMBER 24 ·

*"A light to lighten the Gentiles,
and the glory of thy people Israel."*
Luke 2:32

I f we could look through mighty telescopes or listen to electronic soundings, we could hear and see the metallic stars which both Russia and America have put into space the past few years. None of these synthetic stars have brought peace to the world. But God's star promised peace to the whole world, if man would believe and trust. Too often man's synthetic stars bring fear and anxiety. Our gadget-filled paradise, suspended in a hell of international insecurity, certainly does not offer us the happiness of which the last century dreamed. But there is still a star in the sky. There is still a song in the air. And Jesus Christ is alive. He is with us, a living presence, to conquer despair, to impart hope, to forgive sins, and to take away our loneliness and reconcile us to God.

Prayer For The Day:

Your peace reaches all who love and trust You,
living Lord Jesus. Beloved Savior, I praise Your holy name!

• SEPTEMBER 25 •

"Cleanse me from
this guilt. Let me be pure again."
Psalm 51:2 (TLB)

Guilt is a prominent word among psychoanalysts, psychiatrists, and ministers too. The dictionary calls guilt "the act or state of having done a wrong or committed an offense." The symptoms of guilt are many, but the root cause is one. We have broken the moral law of the universe as expressed in the Ten Commandments and the Sermon on the Mount. So we have a sense of guilt. This guilt causes a variety of psychological problems such as insecurity, tension, hunger for approval, struggles for recognition. A sense of guilt, some psychiatrists point out, is as necessary as a sense of pain. We need both in order to keep us from getting hurt.

Prayer For The Day:

Your Holy Spirit touches my heart
and makes me conscious of my guilt. Forgive me, Lord.

• SEPTEMBER 26 •

"And the Good News about the Kingdom
will be preached throughout the whole world . . ."
Matthew 24:14 (TLB)

We are stewards of the Gospel. The power to proclaim the greatest news in heaven or on earth was not given to the angels. It was given to redeemed men. This was addressed to humble laymen. Some think that only ministers are to preach, but that is wrong. Every Christian is to be a witness; every follower of Christ is to preach the Gospel. We can preach by sharing our experience with others. We can preach by exalting Christ in our daily lives. Sermons which are seen are often more effective than those which are heard. The truth is: the best sermons are both heard and seen. They are a sort of audiovisual testimony. We can also preach by giving to others, so they may preach. Missionary gifts, church offerings, and charitable contributions all speak eloquently of your unselfishness and Christian generosity. In all these things, we are partners with God. We are helping by His grace to redeem the world. God needs our time, our talents, our witnessing, and our money, today more than at any other time in history. Become a full, working, partner with God.

Prayer For The Day:

*Wherever I go today, make me conscious of
the people I meet. They need Your love. So whether
I can speak of You to them, say a kind word or minister
in any way, I would be like You, Lord—ever loving, ever giving.*

•SEPTEMBER 27•

*"Your body is
the home of the Holy Spirit . . ."*
1 Corinthians 6:19 (TLB)

Who is the Holy Spirit? He is God, just as God the Father and God the Son are also God. We speak of them as the Trinity. You ask me to explain the Trinity. Our minds can but dimly grasp these great spiritual facts, because we are finite and God is infinite. It may help to remember that God the Father, God the Son, and God the Holy Spirit have all existed from eternity. The work of creation was given to the Son and we are told that, "All things were made by Him and without Him was not anything made that was made." But when you read the second verse of the first chapter of Genesis, you will find that the Holy Spirit was also there, moving upon the face of His creation. In time, the Son of God came into the world as a man, to redeem the world which He had created. After His death on the cross, and His resurrection, He went back to the Father in heaven. During His earthly ministry His work and life were spent within a circumscribed area in Palestine. When He went back to heaven, He sent the Holy Spirit to exercise a worldwide ministry. Today the Holy Spirit illuminates the minds of people, makes us yearn for God, and takes spiritual truth and makes it understandable to us. All over the world the Holy Spirit is wooing men to Christ, and He lives in the hearts of believers and helps us each day. To be Spirit-filled Christians is to be the kind of Christians that God wants us to be.

Prayer For The Day:

The knowledge of Your Holy Spirit living
in my heart gives me comfort and strength, Lord Jesus.

⋆ SEPTEMBER 28 ⋆

"Before Abraham was, I am."
John 8:58

Jesus did not begin in Bethlehem. The Bible says, "In the beginning was the Word, and the Word was with God, and the Word was God." Jesus said that He existed before the foundation of the world. He was there when the moon and stars were flung out into space from the Father's flaming finger tips. He was there when God created this planet. He has always existed. He is "from everlasting to everlasting."

Prayer For The Day:

You, Lord Jesus, who have always existed,
came down from heaven in love and saved me from the depths
of my sin. In humble adoration I praise You, my Savior and Lord.

⋆ SEPTEMBER 29 ⋆

"Out of his glorious, unlimited
resources he will give you the mighty inner
strengthening of his Holy Spirit."
Ephesians 3:16 (TLB)

Horace Pitkin, the son of a wealthy merchant, was converted and went to China as a missionary. He wrote to his friends in America, saying, "It will be but a short time till we know definitely whether we can serve Him better above or here." Shortly afterward, a mob stormed the gate of the compound where Pitkin defended the women and children. He was beheaded and his head was offered at the shrine of a heathen god, while his body was thrown into a pit with the bodies of nine Chinese Christians. Sherwood

Eddy, writing about him, said, "Pitkin won more men by his death than he ever could have won by his life." Christ needs people today who are made of martyr stuff! Dare to take a strong, uncompromising stand for Him.

Prayer For The Day:

Thank You, Lord, for the examples of those who have gone before us. Help me to take hold of Your unlimited strength, too.

·SEPTEMBER 30·

"I stretch forth my hands unto thee;
my soul thirsteth after thee, as a thirsty land."
Psalm 143:6

Not long ago I visited the dean of a great American university. We looked out the window of his office and watched hundreds of students walking to their classes. I asked the dean, "What is the greatest problem at this university?" He thought a moment and answered, "Emptiness." So many people today are bored, lonely, searching for something. You can see it in their faces. One girl home from college told her wealthy father, "Father, I want something but I don't know what it is." That's true of many people; we want something to meet the deepest problems of our lives, but we haven't found it. David said, "I have found it. I shall not want." The Apostle Paul expressed it, "I have learned in whatever state I am, to be content." You don't have to give up on life, to throw up your hands and cry, "It's no use." . . . You can have God's peace, God's joy, God's happiness, God's security; and yours can become the most thrilling life in the world.

Prayer For The Day:

Lord Jesus, You quench the thirst and longing of my soul. Praise Your blessed name.

·OCTOBER 1·

For the Word of God is
quick, and powerful, and sharper than
any two-edged sword . . ."

Hebrews 4:12

How do we overcome the devil in everyday life? First, we need to recognize that the devil is a defeated foe. The Son of God came to undo the work of the devil. The crucifixion of Christ, which looked like a mighty victory for Satan, turned out to be a great triumph for God, because it was on the cross that Jesus took your sins and my sins. God laid our sins on Christ, so that when our Lord bowed His head and said, "It is finished," He was referring to the plan of redemption and salvation. Then . . . we are to resist the devil. If we resist him, Scripture says, he will flee from us. Jesus overcame the devil not by argument but simply by quoting Scripture. That is why it is so important to learn and memorize Scripture passages.

Prayer For The Day:

Thank You, heavenly Father, for the
protection of Your Word as I face everyday temptations.

·OCTOBER 2·

"He who hath begun a
good work in you will perform it until
the day of Jesus Christ."

Philippians 1:6

Being a Christian is more than just an instantaneous conversion. It is a daily process whereby you grow to be more and more like Christ. When you start out, you start out as a baby. You must be fed on the simple things of the Bible, and you learn to walk in your Christian life gradually. At first you will fall down and make many mistakes, but you are to continue growing. However, there are many people who have stopped growing. They remain spiritual babes all their lives. I am afraid that this experience is all too common today. Perhaps it is yours. Do you remember the day when you gave your heart and life to Christ? You were sure of victory. How easy it seemed to be more than conqueror through Christ who loved you. Thousands of Christians have struggles with themselves. The great need in Christendom today is for Christians to learn the secret of daily victory over sin.

Prayer For The Day:

Father, I fall so many times but
how lovingly You give me Your strength to endure.

•OCTOBER 3•

"He reveals profound mysteries
beyond man's understanding. He knows all
hidden things, for he is light . . ."
Daniel 2:22 (TLB)

The fact of the matter is that science and faith complement each other, and there is no conflict between true science and true religion. Together they give the best foundation for wholesome faith and courage for daily living. When Galileo, the father of modern science, discovered that the earth revolved, instead of the sun moving around the earth, certain religious leaders were greatly disturbed, for they held another theory. But eventually they were reconciled. Since that day we have happily found that true science is compatible with a deep religious faith. So Christianity is what we might term: supra-scientific. There are highways beyond science that lead to truth. Christ Jesus was the Master of spiritual truth, and He imparts these truths to us—as we work out a working relationship with Him.

Prayer For The Day:

Thank You, Father, for the revelation of Your
love when You gave Your beloved Son to die for me.
Nothing science will ever discover will surpass this divine miracle!

•OCTOBER 4•

"And Jesus came and spoke unto them, saying,
All [authority] is given unto me in heaven and in
earth."
Matthew 28:18

Have respect for authority. Jesus Christ was under the authority of His Father in heaven . . . He lived for one thing: to fulfill the will of the Father. Everyone is subject to some kind of authority. There is one chain of command and the ultimate authority at the top is God. What is the authority in your life? Is it your selfishness? Your lust? Your greed? Or have you turned it all over to God and said, "Lord, You are going to be my authority"? When you are under authority, you are then able to assume authority.

Prayer For The Day:

There are still areas in my life
that need to come under Your authority, Lord Jesus.
Give me Your grace and strength to yield everything to You.

•OCTOBER 5•

"Blessed is the man
whom [the Lord] chasteneth . . ."
Psalm 94:12

God sometimes allows Christians to suffer, in order that they might learn the secret of obedience. The Psalmist said, "Before I was afflicted, I went astray; but now have I kept thy Word" (Psalm 119:67). It was not until after great sorrow and much affliction that David learned obedience to God. My dear Christian friend, if you are today suffering at the hand of God and you have asked a thousand times, "Why?" I beg of you to be patient and quiet before God, and listen to the still, small voice. Bow under His loving hand and recognize that above the clouds the sun is shining. God has a purpose and design for your life, and what is happening to you is for your good.

Prayer For The Day:

The human in me says, "Why, Lord?"
whenever I have to bear suffering—but the
Spirit-filled me that was born again says, "I trust You, Father."

·OCTOBER 6·

"Blessed are they which
do hunger and thirst after righteousness; for
they shall be filled."

Matthew 5:6

I t has been my privilege to know what it means to walk in the way of Christ. What a thrilling, joyous experience it is to wake up every morning and know His presence in the room! What a thrilling, joyous experience it is to know in the evening, when the sun is setting, the peace of God as you go to bed and to sleep, and to sleep the sleep of only those who know Christ! What a joy it is to walk in the eternal and permanent experience of Christ! Do you hunger for such a walk? Do you long for such joy, peace, content-ment, abandonment, and adventure in your own soul? If this is your hunger and desire, then God will do exactly what He has promised to do: He will fill you. Every promise God has ever made, He has kept—or will keep.

Prayer For The Day:

Thank You, Lord, for the promise
of filling my life with Your love.

·OCTOBER 7·

". . . this is indeed the Christ,
the Savior of the world."

John 4:42

H istory, philosophy, theology, and—in many centers of learn-ing—even the sciences are being studied to discover what they have to say about Jesus Christ. The records of the Early Church are being reexamined for their testimony to Him. Archaeol-ogists are digging to discover new evidence. Some say that Jesus Christ is a myth, and He never existed in history. Others say that He was merely a man, that there was nothing supernatural about His birth, and that His resurrection was a hallucination. Others talk about a Christless Christianity. Some say that no matter what one thinks about Christ, it does not affect Christianity. They are wrong! Christianity is forever linked with the Person of Christ. Carlyle recognized this when he said, "Had this doctrine of the de-ity of Christ been lost, Christianity would have vanished like a dream." The historian Lecky remarks, "Christianity is not a system of morals, it is the worship of a Person."

Prayer For The Day:

Lord Jesus, You are the
living Christ whom I love and revere.

◆OCTOBER 8◆

"These things I command you,
that ye love one another."

John 15:17

How are we to love? We are to love as God loves us . . . we are to show acceptance and appreciation . . . (to) accept each other as God accepts us. Too many parents refuse to accept and appreciate their children for what they are. That is why a million American children ran away from home last year. A team of Yale researchers has concluded that the majority of these runaways were attempting to escape an unhappy family situation. They yearned to be appreciated. The causes of delinquency, we are told, are broken homes, poverty, lack of recreational facilities, poor physical health, racism, working mothers, and so on . . . The experts never seem to mention the lack of love, or the lack of faith in God. Yet these are the two most important elements for an adolescent's successful maturity. How long has it been since you praised your children instead of criticizing them? David prayed for Solomon and daily praised him, and we are to praise our children daily. Praise your wife. I have found that praise goes a lot further than criticism. Everybody needs to be appreciated.

Prayer For The Day:

It is so easy to criticize
those close to me; but, Lord, give me Your
unreserved love so that they may know
how deeply I appreciate them.

·OCTOBER 9·

"But seek ye
first the kingdom of God . . ."
Matthew 6:33

A man or a woman who has been focusing all attention on financial gains, or business, or social prestige, or who has centered all his affection on some one person, experiences a devastating sense of loss when denied the thing that has given life its meaning. In these tragic moments, the individual recognizes how terribly and completely alone he is. In that moment the Holy Spirit may cause the worldly bandages to fall from his eyes so that he sees clearly for the first time. He recognizes that God is the only source of real power, and the only enduring fountainhead of love and companionship.

Prayer For The Day:

From out of the depths, Lord,
my eyes have seen that only You are unchanging,
eternal love. Help me to put You first in everything I do.

·OCTOBER 10·

"But my God shall supply all
your need according to His riches
in glory by Christ Jesus."
Philippians 4:19

M an hungers for food, and God sends the sun and rain upon the golden fields of grain. The grain is made into flour, and flour into bread, and man's physical hunger is satisfied. Man hungers for love; and God ignites the fire of affection in another heart, and two hearts are made complete in the bonds of holy matrimony. Man hungers for knowledge, and God raises up institutions of learning, calls men to be instructors, puts it into the hearts of the rich to endow them; and men are satisfied in their thirst for knowledge. Man hungers for fellowship; and God allows him to build cities where men can share their industry, and their knowledge, and their skills. Don't tell me that God can supply man with an abundance of everything material and yet will let him starve spiritually! . . . God will satisfy the hunger and thirst of those who desire His righteousness, because He loves the world with an undying affection.

•OCTOBER 11•

*". . . knowing what lies ahead
for you, you won't become bored
with being a Christian . . ."*
Hebrews 6:12 (TLB)

D o you know what nearly all the sociologists say today in their study of young people? The greatest problem facing young people today is not sex—it is boredom, boredom. Did you know that when they had the riot at Hampton Beach in New Hampshire they asked the young people what was wrong, why did they do it? Many of them said, "Just for the hell of it." Bored—life has no purpose, life has no meaning. Give your life to Christ and you will never spend another bored minute.

•OCTOBER 12•

*"Be ye doers of
the Word, and not hearers only . . ."*
James 1:22

J esus indicated that there will be a permissive society just before He comes back. "As in the days of Noah, so shall it be also in the days of the coming of the Son of man." The world today is on an immoral binge such as has not been known since the days of Rome. We are in a hedonistic society, and what we are seeing is human nature expressing itself without God. Many have fallen into an antinomianism in which they believe intellectually, and then go out and live like the devil, imagining that God will forgive them and take them to heaven. I believe there is an obedience to the Gospel, there is a self-denial and a bearing of the cross, if you are to be a follower of Christ. Being a Christian is a serious business.

Prayer For The Day:

*Teach me to deny my selfish desires
and obey Your commandments, Lord Jesus.
Cleanse me so that I might be used to penetrate society
deeply for You.*

·OCTOBER 13·

*". . . believing, ye
rejoice with joy unspeakable . . ."*

1 Peter 1:8

C hrist is the answer to sadness and discouragement. This is a world of thwarted hopes, broken dreams, and frustrated desires. G.K. Chesterton says, "Everywhere there is speed, noise and confusion, but nowhere deep happiness and quiet hearts." A Hollywood columnist wrote about a famous movie star, "The bright, carefree radiance has gone from her pretty face." Optimism and cheerfulness are products of knowing Christ. If the heart has been attuned to God through faith in Christ, then its overflow will be joyous optimism and good cheer. You will never be free from discouragement and despondency until you have been tuned to God. Christ is the wellspring of happiness. He is the fountainhead of joy. Here is the Christian's secret of joy.

Prayer For The Day:

*By Your love I experience the delight of
a quiet heart. Deep down is the joy that cannot be taken
away. Lord, may I always keep my eyes on You, my source of joy.*

·OCTOBER 14·

*"He that walketh
righteously . . . shall dwell on high."*

Isaiah 33:15,16

B eing pure in conduct also includes honesty and integrity in dealing with our fellowmen. A Christian should be known in his neighborhood or place of business as an honest person, a person who can be trusted. Jesus said, "Blessed are the pure in heart." Do you want to be happy? All right, apply this Beatitude to your heart. Take it to yourself. The pure in heart are the only ones who can know what it means to be supremely happy. Their hearts are pure toward God and, as a result are pure toward their fellowmen. They are happy because, in possessing Him who is All and in All, they envy no man's worldly goods. They are happy because they envy not another man's praise. Because they are the enemy of no man, they regard no man as their enemy. The result is peace with God and the world.

Prayer For The Day:

Forgive me, Lord Jesus, my heart is
far from pure. I confess to You all my innermost thoughts.

•OCTOBER 15•

"The words that I speak unto you,
they are spirit, and they are life."

John 6:63

To one of the most religious men of His day, Jesus said, "Ye must be born again" (John 3:7). Nicodemus could not substitute his profound knowledge of religion for spiritual rebirth, and neither can we. I have read a book on water skiing, and it did not take long for me to learn that I could never learn to water ski by reading a book—I would have to experience it. I have read a number of books on golf, but none of them seems to improve my game, I must get out on the golf course and play. You may study theology and religion, but there comes a time when you must experience Christ for yourself.

Prayer For The Day:

Lord, You have given me life and I praise You!

•OCTOBER 16•

"My heart and my flesh crieth
out for the living God."

Psalm 84:2

Loneliness is one of the greatest problems people face today. It is a leading cause of suicide—that is now the third greatest killer of students in the United States. People feel various kinds of loneliness. One of the most common is the loneliness of solitude..

Or there is the loneliness of suffering. Many people experience loneliness in society, or there is the loneliness of sorrow, guilt, and judgment. All of us feel at times a loneliness for God. Someone has called it cosmic loneliness. We don't know what it is. It makes us restless. You see, man was made for God; and without God, he is lonely. But Jesus is knocking at the door of our heart, saying, "I want to come in. Let me in." He doesn't push His way through that door. We have to open it and invite Him in; when we do, He comes in to live forever and we are never lonely again.

Prayer For The Day:

*Lord Jesus, I remember the agony of
my days without You. Lead me to the lonely people
who need to experience the joy of Your companionship, too.*

•OCTOBER 17•

*"Thou wilt keep him in perfect
peace, whose mind is stayed on thee . . ."*

Isaiah 26:3

A re you searching for peace? Are you longing for it? You thought you would find it if you made a lot of money, but you didn't find it. You thought you would find it in getting and accumulating a lot of knowledge, so you got all the degrees you could, but you didn't find it, this peace. You've searched the religions of the world, but you haven't found it. There are a thousand ways you've turned, trying to find peace, but you haven't found it. When you come to Christ by an act of faith, He gives you the Holy Spirit who produces the fruit of the Spirit and gives you the peace that passeth all understanding.

Prayer For The Day:

*Your presence fills my mind with peace, Lord, bringing
into perspective all that I need—You, my heavenly Father.*

•OCTOBER 18•

"I will both lay me down in peace, and sleep:
for thou, Lord, only makest me dwell in safety."
Psalm 4:8

In a materialistic world which has tried to sever diplomatic relations with God, we have nowhere to retreat except within ourselves. We are like turtles in a traffic jam—the best we can do is to pull our heads into our shells and shut our eyes. But that's a good way to get the life crushed out of us, as any dead turtle can attest. Man's conflict with man has been but an expression on the human level of his conflict with God. Until man finds an armistice with God, he cannot know peace with his fellowman. If we are to be peacemakers, we first must make our peace with God.

Prayer For The Day:

In Jesus' name, I have found peace
with You, Father. My soul praises Your holy name.

•OCTOBER 19•

"In the day when I cried, [you]
answered me, and strengthened me . . ."
Psalm 138:3

At some time in life all of us feel the loneliness of sorrow. Mary and Martha were saddened by the death of their brother, Lazarus, and Martha said to Jesus, "If you had been here, my brother would not have died." Theirs was a loneliness of sorrow. The shortest verse in the Bible tells us that at the tomb of Lazarus "Jesus wept." He enters into our sorrows. When we come to Jesus Christ, He does not promise to exempt us from trouble or sorrow. Tears will come, but deep inside there will be a joy that is difficult to explain to you. It is a joy from God—produced by the Holy Spirit. In the midst of trials and agony and tears which come to us all, a supernatural power is given out, producing joy.

Prayer For The Day:

Your comfort in times of sorrow, loving
Lord Jesus, enfolds me, giving light and hope in my darkness.

•OCTOBER 20•

". . . tribulation worketh patience; and patience,
experience; and experience, hope;
and hope maketh not ashamed . . ."
Romans 5:3,4,5

God never promised to remove temptation from us, for even Christ was subject to it. The Bible says that "He was tested in all things, like as we, yet without sin." There is no good reason why you should seek to escape, for such times of testing have beneficial effects. There is a sense of achievement and assurance that results from victory over temptation that cannot come to us otherwise. Temptation shows what people really are. It does not make us Christian or un-Christian. It does make the Christian stronger and causes him to discover resources of power. You can benefit from what might be tragedy, if you will only discover that in just such a time of temptation, Christ can become more real to you than ever, and His salvation will become more meaningful.

Prayer For The Day:

In all times of temptation,
may I remember Your example. Lord Jesus.

•OCTOBER 21•

"Christ in your
hearts is your only hope of glory."
Colossians 1:27 (TLB)

The age-old issue, "Can man save himself, or does he need God?" is still raging across the world as furiously as ever. As long as the world goes on, people will build towers of Babel, fashion their graven images, and invent their own ideologies. Now, as in every period of history, people think they can manage without God. Economically, they may manage; intellectually, they may manage; and socially, they may get by. But down underneath the surface of rational man is a vacuum—a void that can be met only through Jesus Christ. The most astounding fact of all history is that the great and almighty God of heaven can live in your heart. It makes no difference who you are.

Prayer For The Day:

You fill the emptiness and longing
of my soul. I need the presence of Your Spirit, dear Lord.

•OCTOBER 22•

"So it is that we are saved
by faith in Christ and not by the
good things we do."
Romans 3:28 (TLB)

Many people still cling to the notion that man is naturally good. We did not get this from the Greeks. Aristotle said, "There is no good in mankind." We did not get it from Judaism. Jeremiah said, "The heart is deceitful above all things, and desperately wicked; who can know it?" (Jeremiah 17:9). We did not get it from Christian teachings. The Apostle Paul said, "All have sinned, and come short of the glory of God" (Romans 3:23). We got this illusion, I believe, from the philosophers and psychologists of the nineteenth and early twentieth centuries who taught the false doctrine that man is a helpless victim of his environment. The Bible says that man is not naturally good. All human experience confirms it. Man is rebellious by nature. This first rebellion in history happened in the Garden of Eden, where the environment was perfect and there was no heredity on which to blame it!

Prayer For The Day:

Each time I become obsessed
by the idea that my deeds are so noble,
let me remember the magnanimity of Your perfect life.

•OCTOBER 23•

"I appoint unto you a kingdom,
as my Father hath appointed unto me."
Luke 22:29

Many people have asked, "Where is heaven?" We are not told in the Scripture where heaven is. Some students have tried to take some Scriptures and put them together and say that heaven is in the north. They quote Psalm 48:2, "The joy of the whole earth is . . . on the sides of the north . . ." The magnetic needle points north. Perhaps the Celestial City is in the north. We do not know. But no matter where heaven is, it will be where Christ is. Many people ask, "Do you believe that heaven is a literal place?" Yes! Jesus said, "I go to prepare a place for you." The Bible teaches that Enoch and Elijah ascended in a literal body to a literal place that is just as real as Los Angeles, London, or Algiers! The Bible also teaches that heaven will be a place of beauty. It is described in the Bible as "a building of God"—"a city"—"a better country"—"an inheritance"—"a glory." The Bible also indicates that heaven will be a place of great understanding and knowledge of things that we never learned down here.

Prayer For The Day:

Living Lord Jesus, the knowledge
that You have prepared a place for me
in heaven brings comfort and delight to my soul!

•OCTOBER 24•

"Judge not that ye be not judged."
Matthew 7:1

The word *prejudice* means "prejudging" or "making an estimate of others without knowing the facts." Prejudice is a mark of weakness, not of strength. Prejudice is measured by computing the distance between our own biased opinions and the real truth. If we would all be perfectly honest before God, there would be no prejudice.

Prayer For The Day:

You love each one of us
with a love that breaks through
all prejudicial barriers, Father. Forgive me for
the times I judge others. Purify my heart, that I may be
used to draw people together into the bond
of Christ's unifying love.

·OCTOBER 25·

*"Wait on the
Lord, be of good courage . . ."*
Psalm 27:14

Discouragement is nothing new. Many of the great Bible characters became discouraged. Moses in the Sinai desert; Elijah when he heard Jezebel was searching for him to take his life; and David when his son Absalom rebelled against him. It is as old as the history of man. There is often a cause for discouragement. It comes many times when we don't get our way, when things don't work out the way we want them to. Discouragement is the opposite of faith. It is Satan's device to thwart the work of God in your life. Discouragement blinds our eyes to the mercy of God and makes us perceive only the unfavorable circumstances. I have never met anyone who spent time in daily prayer, and in the study of the Word of God, and was strong in faith, who was ever discouraged for very long.

Prayer For The Day:

*Lord, when I am discouraged,
take away the blindness of my wavering
faith. You are with me always. Forgive my ungrateful heart.*

·OCTOBER 26·

*"I am the living bread
that came down from heaven . . ."*
John 6:51

In John 6:48 we read that Jesus said, "I am the bread of life." Jesus had just fed 5,000 people with five loaves and two fishes. They were all excited and thrilled over the great miracle that had occurred, [But] Jesus was talking about something more important than social needs. Bread, in the Scriptures is a symbol of spiritual life. Man has an inborn hunger for God. He cannot be satisfied with anything less than God. God alone can supply the bread which satisfies the inner longing of your soul and the hunger of your heart. . . . The Bible says that He is the Bread of Life.

Prayer For The Day:

Lord Jesus, thank You for
satisfying the yearnings deep down in my
heart. Your presence fulfills the needs of my soul, and I rejoice.

•OCTOBER 27•

"God carefully watches
the goings on of all mankind . . ."

Job 34:21 (TLB)

T here is an old story that tells about a pig. . . . The farmer brought the pig into the house. He gave him a bath, polished his hooves, put some Chanel No. 5 on him, put a ribbon around his neck, and put him in the living room. The pig looked fine. He made a nice and companionable pet for a few minutes. But as soon as the door was opened, the pig left the living room and jumped into the first mud puddle that he could find. Why? Because he was still a pig at heart. His nature had not been changed. He had changed outwardly but not inwardly. . . . You can take a man—dress him up, put him in the front row in church, and he almost looks like a saint. He may fool even his best friends for a while, but then put him in his office, or in the club on Saturday night, and you will see his true nature come out again. Why does he act that way? Because his nature has not been changed. He has not been born again.

Prayer For The Day:

Almighty God, there are times when
I debase my Christian walk and slip again
into the mire. Cleanse and strengthen me, for Jesus' sake.

•OCTOBER 28•

". . . being knit together in love . . ."

Colossians 2:2

T housands of young couples go through with a loveless marriage because no one ever told them what genuine love is. I believe we need to read the 13th chapter of First Corinthians, in which the Apostle Paul gives us a definition of love. He says, "Love is patient and kind; love is not jealous or boastful; it is not arrogant or rude. Love does not insist on its own way; it is not irritable or resentful; it does not rejoice at wrong, but rejoices in the right. Love bears all things, believes all things, hopes all things, endures all things. Love never ends." If people today knew that kind of love, the divorce rate would be sharply reduced.

Prayer For The Day:

Lord Jesus, we need Your love and
forgiveness in our hearts, if we are to love unselfishly.

•OCTOBER 29•

"Let the peace
of God rule in your hearts . . ."
Colossians 3:15

When we examine the problems that confront us in our world today, we find that every one of them resolves into a problem of "inner space," a problem of the dark side of the human spirit. From thousands of letters we receive, it is evident that a large proportion of the population is facing deep personal problems. They vary from person to person, but they do exist, and they are all problems of "inner space." Yes, we are the people who have been conquering outer space, but are in danger of losing the battle of the spirit. But there is a solution—for millions it has already been reached—and that solution is in Jesus Christ. He said "My peace"—my liberty, my freedom—"I give unto you" (John 14:27). Today if we will turn the searchlight of truth on the dark side of our human spirits and let Jesus Christ become the Master Control of our lives, a new day will dawn for us. Submit the "inner space" of your life to Him.

Prayer For The Day:

How often I hurt deep down
inside me, Lord, but the knowledge
of Your love and compassion brings me hope and peace.

·OCTOBER 30·

*"Yea, I have loved thee with
an everlasting love . . ."*

Jeremiah 31:3

A s I read the Bible, I find love to be the supreme and dominant
attribute of God. The promises of God's love and forgiveness are as real, as sure, as positive, as human words can make
them. But the total beauty of the ocean cannot be understood until
it is seen, and it is the same with God's love. Until you actually
experience it, until you actually possess it, no one can describe its
wonders to you. Never question God's great love, for it is as unchangeable a part of God as His holiness. Were it not for the love of
God, none of us would ever have a chance in the future life. But
God is love! And His love for us is everlasting.

Prayer For The Day:

*Knowing myself as I do, Lord, the knowledge
of Your love and forgiveness never ceases to amaze me.
In the knowledge of this, help me to communicate
to others that this love is theirs too, if they will only
reach out for it.*

·OCTOBER 31·

*"For our citizenship is in heaven;
from which also we eagerly wait for a Savior,
the Lord Jesus Christ."*

Philippians 3:20 (NASB)

I f you are moving to a new home, you want to know all about
the community to which you are going. And since we will spend
eternity some place, we ought to know something about it. The
information concerning heaven is found in the Bible. When we talk
about heaven, earth grows shabby by comparison. Our sorrows
and problems here seem so much less, when we have keen anticipation of the future. In a certain sense the Christian has heaven here
on earth. He has peace of soul, peace of conscience, and peace with
God. In the midst of troubles and difficulties he can smile. He has a
spring in his step, a joy in his soul, a smile on his face. But the Bible
also promises the Christian a heaven in the life hereafter.

Father, as I face whatever trials come my way,
I will take heart in the glorious promise of heaven—
knowing I shall be with You!

•NOVEMBER 1•

"You don't understand now
why I am doing it; some day you will."
                                    John 13:7 (TLB)

May I remind you that physical illness is not the worst thing that can happen to you? Some of the most twisted, miserable people I have ever met had no physical handicap. Some of the world's greatest and most useful people have been handicapped. "The Messiah" was composed by Handel, who was suffering from a paralyzed right side and arm. Catherine Booth, in the last year of her life, said that she could not remember one day free from pain. Helen Keller has written, "I thank God for my handicaps, for through them I have found myself, my work, and God." Some of the most radiant Christians I have ever met were "wheelchair" saints. May God give you grace to "triumph in affliction."

Prayer For The Day:

When physical afflictions come into my life,
may they draw me closer to You, my beloved Lord Jesus Christ.

•NOVEMBER 2•

"There is a friend that
sticketh closer than a brother."
                                    Proverbs 18:24

How many lonely people there are today! God did not create man to live in miserable inner loneliness. In that first Eden, God Himself came down to keep the man He had made from being lonely. One of the most heartening things Jesus said to His disciples was, "Lo, I am with you always, even unto the end of the world" (Matthew 28:20). He came to restore fellowship between man and God, and to take away human loneliness. Jesus Christ will take away loneliness from your soul. He will be your companion and friend.

•NOVEMBER 3•

"Keep yourselves in the love of God . . ."

Jude 21

T he Bible is a revelation of the fact that God is love. Many people misunderstand the attribute of God's nature which is love. "God is love" does not mean that everything is sweet, beautiful, and happy, and that God's love could not possibly allow punishment for sin. When we preach justice, it is justice tempered with love. When we preach righteousness, it is righteousness founded on love. When we preach atonement, it is atonement planned by love, provided by love, given by love, finished by love, necessitated because of love. When we preach the resurrection of Christ, we are preaching the miracle of love. When we preach the return of Christ, we are preaching the fulfillment of love. No matter what sin you have committed, or how terrible, dirty, or shameful it may be, God loves you. This love of God is immeasurable, unmistakable, and unending!

Prayer For The Day:

*My heartfelt gratitude to You,
Father, for Your forgiveness and love.
I must be acutely aware that in all my dealing with
others the only yardstick I have is Your immeasurable love.*

•NOVEMBER 4•

*"We started out bad,
being born with evil natures. . . .But God is so
rich in mercy . . . he gave us back our lives again
when he raised Christ from the dead . . ."*

Ephesians 2:3,4 (TLB)

I am reminded of a period when all the agonies that afflict modern minds were felt by another generation, the young people who lived during the first century after Christ. They too sought change, but they directed their efforts at individuals, not at the Roman Empire, not at City Hall. And eventually the whole social and political structure felt their impact. In short, those renewed men and women became filled with a unique dynamic force. Today this same force is available to all people. Over the centuries it has worked in the lives of millions. I personally have seen thousands of people changed. Jesus called it "a new birth." The Scripture tells us that you need not continue as you are. You can become a new person. Whatever your hang-up—guilt, anxiety, fear, hatred—God can handle it.

Prayer For The Day:

I delight in knowing, Lord Jesus,
that there is nothing in my life that is
incapable of being changed through Your redemptive power.

·NOVEMBER 5·

"Whoso trusteth in the Lord, happy is he."
Proverbs 16:20

T here is much in our nature that perplexes us. Many people are disturbed as they confront the troubling riddle of their own existence. They are bewildered by their proneness to sin and evil. They quake and tremble at the thought of their inability to cope with their own lives. Christ can give you satisfying answers to such questions as "Who am I?" "Why was I born?" "What am I doing here?" "Where am I going?" All of the great questions of life can be measured when you come by faith to Jesus Christ and receive Him as your Lord. Let Him be your Pilot. He can take away the worry from your life.

Prayer For The Day:

I trust You, Lord, to control my life.
Knowing You will guide me in the right path gives me joy.

•NOVEMBER 6•

*"But they that wait upon
the Lord shall renew their strength . . ."*

Isaiah 40:31

It is an exhilarating experience to live the new life, with Christ inside me enabling me to live it. As a man was riding along in his Ford, suddenly something went wrong. He got out and looked at the engine, but he could find nothing wrong. As he stood there, another car came in sight, and he waved it down to ask for help. Out of a brand-new Lincoln stepped a tall, friendly man who asked, "Well, what's the trouble?" "I cannot get this Ford to move," was the reply. The stranger made a few adjustments under the hood and then said, "Now start the car." When the motor started, its grateful owner introduced himself and then asked, "What is your name, sir?" "My name," answered the stranger, "is Henry Ford." The one who made the Ford knew how to make it run. God made you and me, and He alone knows how to run your life and mine. We could make a complete wreck of our lives without Christ. When He is at the controls, all goes well. Without Him, we can do nothing.

Prayer For The Day:

*Lord, so often I forget to
give You complete control and I fail.
Teach me to rely completely on You for my strength and needs.*

•NOVEMBER 7•

*"Let us love one another; for love is of God;
and every one that loveth is born of God, and
knoweth God. . . . And this commandment
have we from him, that he who loveth
God love his brother also."*

1 John 4:7,21

If you would know the measure of your love for God, just observe your love for your fellowman. Our compassion for others is an accurate gauge of our devotion to God. Some time ago, with some friends, I went through a museum in San Francisco. Among other things, we saw a collection of instruments of torture which were employed by religious people to force other people to believe as they did. History is largely the record of man's inhumanity to man.

Prayer For The Day:

> *Lord God, fill my heart that*
> *I may love with the compassion of Jesus.*

•NOVEMBER 8•

> *"The Lord thy God in the midst of thee is*
> *mighty; he will save, he will rejoice over thee*
> *with joy . . ."*
> *Zephaniah 3:17*

The world's millions could come down to the beach and reach out their hands to be filled with sea water. They could each take as much as they wanted, as much as they needed—and still the ocean would remain unchanged. Its might and power would be the same, the life in its unfathomable depths would continue unaltered, although it had supplied the needs of every single person standing with outstretched hands along its shores. So it is with God. He can be everywhere at once, heeding the prayers of all who call out in the name of Christ; performing the mighty miracles that keep the stars in their places, and the plants bursting up through the earth, and the fish swimming in the sea. There is no limit to God. There is no limit to His wisdom. There is no limit to His power. There is no limit to His love. There is no limit to His mercy.

Prayer For The Day:

> *Almighty God, how glorious are my*
> *thoughts of You, for You are everywhere—*
> *loving and caring for the minutest details of our lives!*

•NOVEMBER 9•

> *"Having a good conscience . . ."*
> *1 Peter 3:16*

What is conscience? God has put within each one of us something that cries aloud against us, whenever we do that which we know to be wrong. Conscience is the detective that watches the direction of our steps and decries every conscious transgression. Conscience is a vigilant eye before which each imagination, thought, and act, is held up for either censure or approval. I believe there is no greater argument for the existence of God in the world today than conscience. There is no greater proof of the existence of a moral law and Lawgiver in the universe than this little light of the soul. It is God's voice to the inner man. Conscience is our wisest counselor and teacher, our most faithful and most patient friend.

Prayer For The Day:

Thank You, Father, for my conscience
which checks me and guards my actions. Help me
to be alert to its promptings, through Your Holy Spirit.

•NOVEMBER 10•

"Your faith should not stand
in the wisdom of men, but in the power of God."
1 Corinthians 2:5

The word "mystery" is used many times in Scripture. Some of the mysteries of the past have been fathomed by science. Others still bewilder mankind. This fact remains: All of the garnered wisdom of the ages is only a scratch on the surface of man's search for the knowledge of the universe. For the most part, God retains His secrets, and man standing on his intellectual tiptoes can comprehend only a small fraction of the Lord's doings. This inability to comprehend fully the mysteries of God does not in any way curtail the Christian faith. On the contrary, it enhances our belief. We do not understand the intricate pattern of the stars in their courses, but we know that He who created them does, and that just as surely as He guides them, He is charting a safe course for us. A "mystery" in Scripture is a previously hidden truth now divinely revealed, but in which a supernatural element remains unknown despite the revelation.

Prayer For The Day:

Just as You have guided all who love You
in the past, I know my life is being lovingly
directed. My faith is small but, God, You are my strength.

•NOVEMBER 11•

"For we know not what we should
pray for as we ought; but the Spirit himself
maketh intercession for us with
groanings which cannot
be uttered."

Romans 8:26

John Knox, with an all-consuming soul-concern for his country, prayed, "Give me Scotland, or I die!" His earnest travail was rewarded with a spiritual rebirth in his land. This is what is termed "praying in the Spirit." It is the manifestation of a deep spiritual concern for others, and it is instilled by the Spirit of God. This kind of prayer can leap over oceans, speed across burning deserts, spring over mountains, bound through jungles, and carry the healing, helping power of the Gospel to the object of prayer. That "the Spirit Himself maketh intercession" indicates that it is actually God pleading, praying, and mourning through us. Thus we become co-laborers with God, actual partners with Him; our lives are lifted from the low plane of selfishness to the high plane of creativeness with God. John Knox travailed, and the Church in Scotland broke into new life.

Prayer For The Day:

My heart's cry is heard—thank You, Lord Jesus!

•NOVEMBER 12•

"In the world ye shall have tribulation: but
be of good cheer; I have overcome the world."

John 16:33

You should not expect the easy way, for if you do you are certainly destined for disappointment. Any person who knows the Bible knows that the Christian life is likened to an athletic contest or to warfare, and neither one is easy. Jesus warned His followers to count carefully the cost, and that certainly does not speak of an easy way. But there is no good thing that comes without cost. The Christian life is the most satisfying, but only when we actually go all out and all the way. It is the Christian who tries to compromise who finds life miserable, for he has all the problems, without the fellowship that comes through surrender.

For every trial and test, Christ supplies an abundance of grace with which to bear it, and in our weakness we are made strong.

Prayer For The Day:

Let me never look for the easy way
when You, Lord Jesus, gave everything for me

•NOVEMBER 13•

"I beg you to keep away from the evil
pleasures of this world . . ."

1 Peter 2:11 (TLB)

We all know there is no such thing as absolute freedom. We cannot drive down the street at 100 miles an hour. You can't swing your fist at me, because your freedom stops at the end of my nose. We can say that we want freedom to publish pornography, to push harmful drugs, to have unrestricted sex, to lie, to cheat; but if we continue with that kind of permissive freedom, we shall destroy ourselves. Man can remain free only so long as he has the moral power to restrain his appetites. Basically, our problem is heart trouble. Our hearts need to be changed . . . peace will never come until we have changed human nature, until people begin loving each other instead of hating each other.

Prayer For The Day:

I need Your guidelines in my life, Lord.
Loving You frees me from the bondage of my carnal appetite.

•NOVEMBER 14•

". . . but as for me and
my house, we will serve the Lord."

Joshua 24:15

The basic unit of any society is the home. When the home begins to break, the society is on the way to disintegration. Thousands of homes are almost on the rocks. Many couples are fearful lest their home, too, will be broken some day. There is one great insurance policy that you can take out, in order to guarantee the unity and happiness of your home. It is simple: Make Christ the center of your home. A home is like a solar system. The center, the great sun, holds the solar system together. If it were not for the sun, the solar system would fly to pieces. Unless the Son of God is put at the center of your home, it, too, may fly to pieces.

Prayer For The Day:

> *How easy it is to push You to one side,*
> *Lord, and superficially remember Your blessings.*
> *May we always keep You at the center of all that we do*
> *in our homes.*

•NOVEMBER 15•

> *"Yet of myself I will not glory,*
> *but in mine infirmities."*
> *2 Corinthians 12:5*

D r. Edward Judson, in speaking of the life of his father, Adoniram Judson, at the dedication of the Judson Memorial Church in New York City, said, "Suffering and success go together. If you are succeeding without suffering, it is because others before you have suffered; if you are suffering without succeeding, it is that others after you may succeed." Happy are they that mourn. They can be happy because they know that their pain, their distress, and their privation are the travail of a new creation, the birthpangs of a better world. They can be happy if they are aware that the Master Artist, God, is employing both light and shadow to produce a masterpiece worthy of divine artistry. They can also glory in their infirmities, smile through their tears, and sing in the midst of their sorrow, because they realize that in God's economy, "If we suffer, we shall also reign with Him."

Prayer For The Day:

> *In suffering I will learn to praise You, loving Savior.*

•NOVEMBER 16•

> *"The foundation of God standeth sure . . ."*
> *2 Timothy 2:19*

O n campus the quickest way to security is through the crowd. Precisely where students talk about being independent and on their own, you will find them practicing the most rigid conformity in dress, in speech, in moral attitudes, and in thinking. Sometimes they follow fashion at the expense of integrity. They dread to be alone. They do not want to stand out or be different. They want to conform. After they graduate from college, many of these young people want nothing more than a good job with a big firm, and a home somewhere in suburbia. But they don't find security then either. Only Jesus Christ can give you the security that you are looking for.

Prayer For The Day:

Long-sought-after security I found
only in Your abiding love, my Savior, Jesus Christ.

•NOVEMBER 17•

"Those things, which ye have both learned, and
received, and heard, and seen in me, do . . ."
Philippians 4:9

Integrity is the glue that holds our way of life together. What our young people want to see in their elders is integrity, honesty, truthfulness, and faith. What they hate most of all is hypocrisy and phoniness. That is why it is important for us to go to church, to read the Bible, and to say grace at the table. Let them see us doing what we would like them to do.

Prayer For The Day:

Take away the "front," Father,
that so often creeps into my life. I would live
in such a way that young people will be drawn to You, too.

•NOVEMBER 18•

"Let this mind be in you,
which was also in Christ Jesus."
Philippians 2:5

It is impossible to live pure lives until we have pure hearts. Many people today are trying to put the cart before the horse. They are teaching purity of motives, desires, and actions to old, deceitful hearts! No wonder we have ended up such moral failures, in spite of our vaunted knowledge and psychological approaches. Pure motives, desires, and actions stem from pure hearts. Pure hearts will be Christlike. It is God's desire that we be conformed to the image of His Son. If Christ lives within us and our bodies become the abode of the Holy Spirit, is it any wonder that we should be like Him?

Prayer For The Day:

Cleanse my heart and make
it the home of Your Spirit, Lord.

·NOVEMBER 19·

"Keep a close watch on all you do
and think. Stay true to what is right . . ."
1 Timothy 4:16 (TLB)

In searching for ways to bridge the generation gap, there is no doubt that we, as parents, will have to practice what we preach, by striving more and more to bring our conduct into line with our code of beliefs. No mother can demand that her daughter abstain from sleeping around when she herself is flirting and on occasion compromising her own moral conduct. No father, who wavers between heavy social drinking and occasional binges to the edge of alcoholism, and who can't speak a pleasant word in the morning until he has had a cigarette, can yell incessantly at his son to get off marijuana, the route that often leads to hard drugs. Consistency, constancy, and undeviating diligence to maintain Christian character are a must if the older generation is to command respect, or even a hearing, from the young.

Prayer For The Day:

Younger eyes see my errant behavior, Lord. Help me
to be the right example—one which will draw them to You.

·NOVEMBER 20·

"The one who is the true Light arrived to
shine on everyone coming into the world."
John 1:9 (TLB)

The world is stumbling in darkness from one crisis to another. The crises are getting worse and worse, and are coming closer and closer to home. Inflation, population explosion, hunger, dominate vast areas of the world. Jesus said, "I am the light of the world. You follow me and give your life to me and I'll take you out of the darkness of this world, out of this confusion, out of this mess that you're in, and I'll give you peace and joy. A light will burn in your heart and mind that you never had before. I will command the light to come on in your life."

Prayer For The Day:

Your light shines in the
darkest place and gives me hope, Lord Jesus.

•NOVEMBER 21•

". . . ye might have life through his name."
John 20:31

"**I**s life worth living?" To scores of people life has ceased to be worth living. To all of you I have good news. God did not create you to be a defeated, discouraged, frustrated, wandering soul, seeking in vain for peace of heart and peace of mind. He has bigger plans for you. He has a larger orb and a greater life for you. The answer to your problem, however great, is as near as your Bible, as simple as first-grade arithmetic, and as real as your heartbeat. Upon the authority of God's Word, I tell you that Christ is the answer to every baffling perplexity which plagues mankind. In Him is found the cure for care, a balm for bereavement, a healing for our hurts, and a sufficiency for our insufficiency.

Prayer For The Day:

Teach me, Lord, as today
I read Your Word, that the life
You would have me live is one of joy and fulfillment.

•NOVEMBER 22•

"I am come that they might have life,
and that they might have it more abundantly."
John 10:10

Do you think that God would have bothered to send His Son to the world, if man had been able to face life and eternity alone? Christ's coming to the world proved that God was not happy with man's unhappiness. He sent Him not only that we might have eternal life but that we might have life here and now, and that we might have it more abundantly—Life with a capital L! Jesus' teaching was unique and different. He took religion out of the theoretical category and placed it in the practical. He spoke with authority! He spoke with finality! He spoke as though He knew . . . and He did! His was not the soft empty conjecture of the philosopher, who professes to search for truth—but readily admits he has never found it. It was more the confident voice of the mathematician who gives his answers unhesitatingly, because the proof of the answers can be found within the problem.

Prayer For The Day:

> *Almighty God, You have given me real*
> *life through Jesus Christ. My soul praises You.*

•NOVEMBER 23•

> *"He that eateth, eateth*
> *to the Lord; for he giveth God thanks . . ."*
> *Romans 14:6*

I t is the custom of many Christians to bow their heads in public places and give thanks for the food that has been placed before them. I have had scores of waiters and waitresses tell me that when we bowed our heads, it was the first time they had ever seen that happen in their restaurant. Millions never pause to give a word of thanks to God for the food provided. Few homes have a moment of thanksgiving at the beginning of the meal or at any other time of the day. Even at Thanksgiving time only a minority will pause and give thanks to God. Thanksgiving is recognition of a debt that cannot be paid. We express thanks, whether or not we are able otherwise to reimburse the giver. When thanksgiving is filled with true meaning and is not just the formality of a polite "thank you," it is the recognition of dependence.

Prayer For The Day:

> *Lord God, I know that I am*
> *completely dependent upon You.*
> *Thank You for daily providing all that my body needs.*

·NOVEMBER 24·

*"O give thanks unto the Lord,
for he is good: because his mercy
endureth for ever."*

Psalm 118:1

This year, as we observe our season of thanksgiving, let us be grateful not only in word but also in deed. Let our gratitude find expression in a resolve to live a life more unselfish and more consecrated to Jesus Christ. When we sit around our tables laden with sumptuous delicacies, let us not forget that half the world will go to bed hungry. As we enjoy the comforts of our cozy homes, let us not forget that great numbers in other parts of the world have no homes to go to. When we step into our sleek automobiles, let us not forget that most of the people in the world cannot afford even a bicycle. In the Lord's Prayer as recorded in the sixth chapter of Matthew, we read, "Give us this day our daily bread." Scripture teaches that the good things of this life are the gifts of God, and that He is the donor of all our blessings. Thanksgiving? Yes. Let us get on our knees humbly and thank God for the blessings He has given us, both material and spiritual. They have come from His hands.

Prayer For The Day:

*You bring me such abundance,
almighty God. As I think of Thanksgiving
Day, may my heart be completely consecrated to Your Son,
Jesus Christ, so that through Him my life will show
my gratitude to You.*

·NOVEMBER 25·

*"To us there is but one God, the Father . . .
and one Lord Jesus Christ . . ."*

1 Corinthians 8:6

Ultimately, in one way or another, or at one time or another, we shall be faced with this question: What think ye of Christ? Whose Son is He? If Jesus Christ is not who He claimed to be, He is a deceiver, or an egomaniac. We must answer this question with both belief and action. We must not only believe something about Jesus, but we must do something about Him. We must accept Him, or reject Him. Jesus made clear who He was, and why He came into the world. He asked His disciples, "Whom do men say that I, the Son of man, am?" They told Him of a variety of designations on the human level. Then Jesus turned to them and asked, "But whom say ye that I am?" Whereupon Peter replied with his historic affirmation, "Thou art the Christ, the Son of the living God" (Matthew 16:13-16). This is the apex of faith. This is the pinnacle of belief. This is where the faith of each must rest if he hopes for salvation. Christ is inescapable! You, too, must decide, "What shall I do with Christ?"

Prayer For The Day:

You are the Christ, Lord Jesus, Son of
the living God! In adoration I worship You—my Redeemer.

•NOVEMBER 26•

"Now you are happy with the inexpressible
joy that comes from heaven itself . . ."
1 Peter 1:8 (TLB)

Christians are to enjoy life and enjoy one another. When children see no joy in their home, no joy in your Christianity, they will not be attracted by it. When they see you excited about going to a ball game, or watching television, and then dragging around to do spiritual things, they will soon get the idea that Christianity does not mean much to you. Your attitude will rub off. My wife says that the best way to get a child to eat his food is to see his parents enjoying theirs. Our children will not be attracted to Christ if we make Him seem dull.

Prayer For The Day:

May I live so close to You,
Jesus, that those around me will see Your joy.

•NOVEMBER 27•

"Casting down imaginations . . .
and bringing into captivity every thought
to the obedience of Christ."

2 Corinthians 10:5

Thousands of people have made plans to escape from the realities of life. A new word has come into common usage the last few years. That word is "escapism." The dictionary defines it as "a retreat from reality into an imaginary world." The escape of imagination. Solomon spoke of the unregenerate heart as one which is inclined to excessive fantasy. The dream world Satan promotes always ends with disillusionment. Thousands of people live in an unreal dream world, while shirking their responsibilities toward their families and toward God. The Bible teaches that with Christ in your heart, you can face the realities of life. Even though they are hard, the grace of God will give you greater joy and pleasure than any dream world to which you try to escape.

Prayer For The Day:

Lord, so often my thoughts make
a wasteland of what You are wanting to plant there.
This day let every one of them be captive to Your leading.

•NOVEMBER 28•

"The Lord is close to those whose hearts are
breaking; he rescues those who are humbly sorry for
their sins."

Psalm 34:18 (TLB)

In God's economy, you must go down into the valley of grief before you can scale the heights of spiritual glory. You must become tired and weary of living alone before you seek and find the fellowship of Christ. You must come to the end of "self" before you can begin to live. The happiest day of my life was when I realized that my own ability, my own goodness, and my own morality were insufficient in the sight of God. I am not exaggerating when I say that my mourning was turned to joy, and my sighing into singing. Happy are they that mourn for the inadequacy of self, for they shall be comforted with the sufficiency of God.

Prayer For The Day:

Lord Jesus, I know that apart from You
I can do nothing of lasting value. Help me to come
to the end of self and allow You to control the reins of my life.

•NOVEMBER 29•

"In whom we have redemption . . .
the forgiveness of sins."

Ephesians 1:7

S atan is at work in our world. The Bible is my authority. He exists and he has control over thousands of young people, whose hearts have never been captured by Jesus Christ. He has hundreds of agents writing pornographic literature and producing sex movies to pollute young minds. He has intellectuals in high positions teaching a hedonistic and permissive philosophy. Daily I come in contact with mixed-up people who are caught in the anguish of their own unpreparedness, intellectuals who have been seduced by false science, and rich men who are held in the grip of insecurity. They have no commitment to any goal. They lack an anchor for their real self. And I long to take every one of them by the hand and lead them into the presence of the One who said, "Come unto me, all ye that labor and are heavy laden, and I will give you rest."

Prayer For The Day:

So many without You, Lord! Use me to
lead others from a destructive course
to the one which will give them the satisfaction
that only You can give.

•NOVEMBER 30•

"That I may know him, and
the power of his resurrection, and the
fellowship of his sufferings . . ."

Philippians 3:10

W. C. Burns of India wrote, "Oh to have a martyr's heart, if not a martyr's crown." Popularity and adulation are far more dangerous for the Christian than persecution. It is easy, when all goes smoothly, to lose our sense of balance and our perspective. The important thing is to walk with Christ, to live for Christ, and to have one consuming passion—to please Him. Then, whatever happens, we know that He has permitted it in order to teach us some priceless lesson and to perfect us for His service. He will enrich our circumstances, be they pleasant or disagreeable, by the fact of His presence with us.

Prayer For The Day:

Lord, my soul wants to love
and know You far more deeply. Forgive the
times I have set my eyes on things that keep me from You.

·DECEMBER 1·

"There is sin in their homes, and
they are polluted to the depths of their souls.
But I will call upon the Lord to
save me—and he will."
Psalm 55:15,16 (TLB)

The broken home has become the number one social problem of America, and could ultimately lead to the destruction of our civilization. Since the basic unit of any society is the home, when the home begins to break, the society is on the way to disintegration. It is a threat to the American way of life. It does not make screaming headlines; but, like termites, it is eating away at the heart and core of the American structure. It is high time that our so-called experts on marriage, the family, and the home turn to the Bible. We have read newspaper columns and listened to counselors on the radio; psychiatrists have had a land-office business. In it all, the One who performed the first marriage in the Garden of Eden and instituted the union between man and wife has been left out.

Prayer For The Day:

I pray, Lord, for the homes in this beloved country.
Without your love and wisdom guiding us,
our society will crumble.

·DECEMBER 2·

*"Said I not unto thee, that, if thou wouldest
believe, thou shouldest see the glory of God?"*
John 11:40

I f you are a young man or young woman hooked on dissent or despair, ready to split, then lend me your attention. My answer concerns your dreams, and the element in your make-up called "faith." All that God requires of anyone in taking his first step toward Him and toward total self-fulfillment is faith—faith in His Word, that teaches that God loves you and that you were alienated from Him by sin, that Jesus Christ died on the cross for you, that when you make a personal surrender to Him as Lord and Savior, He can transform you from the inside out.

Prayer For The Day:

*Your Word, heavenly Father, brings
me hope and redemption through Jesus Christ—
thrusts through the despondencies of life and says You love me!*

·DECEMBER 3·

"Let love be your greatest aim . . ."
1 Corinthians 14:1 (TLB)

W hat about love? How can you be certain you're in love? I suggest these simple measures that you can apply to yourself. Is your love patient? Is it considerate? Can it wait until marriage for physical fulfillment? Experience says that true love's patience is inexhaustible. True love does not assert itself, claim rights, or demand privileges. It always thinks first of the other person. The biblical phrase is it "vaunteth not itself." True love never thinks evil of the beloved. It is never suspicious, but always supportive and inspiring. True love bears all things. Nothing weakens or undermines it. It is a rock, an anchor, a foundation for all the years to come. These simple tests are a mirror that millions have used. Physiologists, psychiatrists, and marriage counselors attest their validity. They were first recommended almost two thousand years ago by a man named Paul, in 1 Corinthians, chapter 13. That chapter provides the finest definition of love the world has received.

Prayer For The Day:

*Your limitless love causes me to see the
narrowness of mine, Lord Jesus. Fill me with Your loving Spirit.*

·DECEMBER 4·

*"When your patience is finally
in full bloom, then you will be ready for
anything, strong in character . . ."*
James 1:4 (TLB)

This is a high-strung, neurotic, impatient age. We hurry when there is no reason to hurry—just to be hurrying. This fast-paced age has produced more problems and less morality than previous generations, and it has given all of us jangled nerves. Impatience has produced a new crop of broken homes, or more new ulcers, and has set the stage for more world wars.

Prayer For The Day:

*May my heart be still amid all the turmoil,
as I remember Your patience with me, Lord Jesus.*

·DECEMBER 5·

*"I sought the Lord, and he heard me,
and delivered me from all my fears."*
Psalm 34:4

Man has always been beset by worry, and the pressures of modern life have aggravated the problem. To men of all time Jesus said, "Take therefore no thought for the morrow . . . but seek ye first the kingdom of God, and His righteousness; and all these things shall be added unto you" (Matthew 6:33-34). Many of you are filled with a thousand anxieties. Bring them to Jesus Christ by faith. He will bring peace to your soul and your mind.

Prayer For The Day:

*Knowing You hear me, Lord, as I talk with You brings me peace in
the midst of any storm.*

·DECEMBER 6·

*"Yet not I, but the grace of God
which was with me."*
1 Corinthians 15:10

L et us face this fact: We came into the world with nothing, and we will leave it with nothing. Where do we get the notion that man's idea of success and God's are the same? You have written a book; you are a clever manager and promoter; you are a talented artist; you are independently rich; you have achieved fame and fortune. Without the gifts of intelligence, imagination, personality, and physical energy—which are all endowed by God—where would you be? Are we not born poor? Do we not die poor? And would we not be poor indeed without God's infinite mercy and love? We came out of nothing; and if we are anything, it is because God is everything. If He were to withhold His power for one brief instant from us, if He were to hold in check the breath of life for one moment, our physical existence would shrivel into nothingness, and our souls would be whisked away into an endless eternity. Those who are poor in spirit recognize their creatureliness and their sinfulness—but more, they are ready to confess their sins and renounce them.

Prayer For The Day:

*All I have or am, Lord God,
has been given to me by Your almighty
hands. Forgive me when I tend to boast about my
own accomplishments—for I am nothing without
your grace and love.*

·DECEMBER 7·

*". . . we can come to the Lord with
perfect assurance and trust . . ."*
1 John 3:21 (TLB)

T he Bible teaches that faith will manifest itself in three ways. It will manifest itself in doctrine—in what you believe. It will manifest itself in worship—your communion with God and the fellowship of the church. It will manifest itself in morality—in the way you live and behave . . . The Bible also teaches that faith does not end with trust in Christ for your salvation. Faith continues.

Faith grows. It may be weak at first, but it will become stronger as you begin to read the Bible, pray, go to church, and experience God's faithfulness in your Christian life. You will learn more and more how to rely on Christ for every need, in meeting every circumstance, and every trial.

Prayer For The Day:

Your Word teaches how greatly
You desire for me to rely on Your love
and strength. I praise Your name, my Lord and my Redeemer.

·DECEMBER 8·

"Let us therefore come
boldly unto the throne of grace . . ."
Hebrews 4:16

Praying is simply a two-way conversation between you and God. Thousands of people pray only when they are under great stress, or in danger, overcome by uncertainty. I have been in airplanes when an engine died; then people started praying. I have talked to soldiers who told me that they never prayed until they were in the midst of battle. There seems to be an instinct in man to pray in times of trouble. We know "there are no atheists in foxholes," but the kind of Christianity that fails to reach into our everyday lives will never change the world. Develop the power of prayer. Man is more powerful when he is in prayer than when he is behind the most powerful guns. A nation is more powerful when it unites in earnest prayer to God than when its resources are channeled into defensive weapons. The answers to all our problems can be had through contact with almighty God.

Prayer For The Day:

My time spent in prayer with You,
dear Lord, is the highlight of my day. To know
You are waiting to have this communion humbles me.
Yet You say I can come boldly—this I do now,
knowing You hear me!

·DECEMBER 9·

*"The Word was made
flesh . . . full of grace and truth."*

John 1:14

On the cover of your Bible and my Bible appear the words "Holy Bible." Do you know why the Bible is called holy? Why should it be called holy when so much lust and hate and greed and war are found in it? It is because the Bible tells the truth. It tells the truth about God, about man, and about the devil. The Bible teaches that we exchange the truth of God for the devil's lie about sex, for example; and drugs, and alcohol, and religious hypocrisy. Jesus Christ is the ultimate truth. Furthermore, He told the truth. Jesus said that He was the truth, and the truth would make us free.

Prayer For The Day:

*Almighty God, I thank
You for the truth which You have
given me through Your beloved Son, Jesus Christ.*

·DECEMBER 10·

*"Your steadfast love, O Lord,
is as great as all the heavens . . ."*

Psalm 36:5 (TLB)

Young people talk a lot about love. Most of their songs are about love . . . "The supreme happiness of life," Victor Hugo said long ago, "is the conviction that we are loved." "Love is the first requirement for mental health," declared Sigmund Freud. The Bible teaches that "God is love" and that God loves you. To realize that is of paramount importance. Nothing else matters so much. And loving you, God has a wonderful plan for your life. Who else could plan and guide your life so well?

Prayer For The Day:

*In knowing I am loved by You,
almighty God, my heart trusts You to guide me.*

•DECEMBER 11•

"Whosoever shall deny me before men,
him will I also deny before my Father . . ."
Matthew 10:33

What is idolatry? Idolatry is anything that comes between us and God. Joshua told his people that their nation would be destroyed if they persisted in idolatry, and their souls would suffer eternal death. He said, "You must make your decision today. You must decide whether you want to serve the idols of this life, or the living God." "Choose you this day," said Joshua, "as for me and my house, we will serve the Lord." What about you? Are you taking your stand with Joshua? No matter what the cost? I am asking you to choose this day whom you will serve. Our families cannot choose Christ for us. Our friends cannot do it. God is a great God, but even God can't make the decision for us. He can help, but only we can decide. We have to make our own choice.

Prayer For The Day:

Lord Jesus Christ, take
away the idols in my life so that,
completely undivided, I may serve You, my Savior.

•DECEMBER 12•

"And the Lord make you to increase
and abound in love one toward another,
and toward all men . . ."
1 Thessalonians 3:12

One of the growing psychological problems facing people to-day is loneliness. One of the greatest ministries that a person can have today is just being a good listener. Many people are longing not only to be loved but to have someone who will listen to them. When we love God with all our hearts, then we have the capacity to love our neighbor. The greatest need in the world today is not more science, not more social engineering, not more teaching, not more knowledge, not more power, not even more preaching—the greatest need we have today is for *love*. And the only way that love can be supplied is by a supernatural act of the Holy Spirit that transforms lives. The love that God gives is not the ordinary love that we find in the world today. When we love our neighbors, it is not our loving with natural love, it God loving through us. If you are willing to do this, God will give you His love.

Prayer For The Day:

> *I love You, Jesus. How often I take for*
> *granted Your immeasurable act of love for me*
> *upon the cross. Help me to keep my eyes fixed on You,*
> *that through Your supreme example I can reach out*
> *to my neighbor.*

•DECEMBER 13•

> *"With everlasting kindness*
> *will I have mercy on thee, saith*
> *the Lord thy Redeemer."*
>
> Isaiah 54:8

If God is all-powerful and all-loving, it would seem inconsistent with His nature to allow anyone to be lost. Here again we rationalize because we do not understand the nature of God. God cannot go against His own laws and against His own nature. God is holy. He cannot tolerate sin in His presence. He created us free to choose how we would live. He invites us to come His way, but leaves us free to pursue our own ends with tragic, natural consequences. We glibly say, "Surely a loving God would not allow a person He loves to be lost. He just wouldn't allow it." Far from allowing it, God has done everything He can to prevent it! Talk about love! "God so loved the world, that He gave His only begotten Son . . ." This is good news. Because of what God in love has done for us, we need not be lost.

Prayer For The Day:

> *Almighty God, your magnanimous*
> *love is felt in my life, as I live each day*
> *through the grace of Your Son, Jesus Christ.*

•DECEMBER 14•

*"If we ask anything according to his
will, he heareth us."*

1 John 5:14

God has said, "If my people . . . pray . . . then will I hear from heaven." Before three thousand people were brought into the Church on the day of Pentecost, the disciples had spent ten days in prayer, fasting, and spiritual travail. God desires that Christians be concerned and burdened for a lost world. If we pray this kind of prayer, an era of peace may come to the world and the hordes of wickedness may be turned back.

Prayer For The Day:

*Almighty God, burden my heart for those in
the world who have not experienced Your peace in their lives.*

•DECEMBER 15•

*"Let no man despise thy youth; but be thou
an example of the believers . . ."*

1 Timothy 4:12

Lord Chesterton once said, "I believe in bedside repentance, but I do not want to depend upon it." During a serious illness a person's mind does not function normally. Getting right with God is something one should do in the bloom of health. However, as far as the Lord is concerned, "His ear is not heavy that He cannot hear, nor His arm shortened that He cannot save." He loves us equally, in sickness or in health; while we are living, or while we are dying. In my experience, I have not known of too many people who found Christ on their deathbed. When we come to Christ in our youth, a life is saved. When we come in old age, a soul is salvaged and life eternal is assured; but the opportunity to live a life for Christ has been lost.

Prayer For The Day:

*Lord God, burden my heart to
reach out to the young persons starting their
adventure in life—and the old persons dreading the end
of their journey. Let me tell them the message
of Your saving love.*

·DECEMBER 16·

*"God will tenderly comfort
you when you undergo these same
sufferings . . ."*

2 Corinthians 1:7 (TLB)

This question, "Why must the righteous suffer?" is as old as time. There is only one place that we can find an answer, and that is in the Bible. You do not need to study the Scriptures long to learn why sinners meet reverses and anguish. They are apart from God. Their sorrow is the result of their sins. But—why do Christians suffer? Scripture teaches that many Christians suffer so that they may fellowship with others who are in affliction. Only those who have known sorrow and suffering can have fellowship with those in affliction. The Word of God also teaches that Christians suffer in order that they might glorify God in their lives. The Bible further teaches that Christians suffer in order that God might teach them lessons in prayer. Also, Christians suffer in order that God might bring them to repentance.

Prayer For The Day:

*How tender is Your comfort,
Lord. How loving Your chastening.*

·DECEMBER 17·

*"Hatred stirreth up strifes:
but love covereth all sins."*

Proverbs 10:12

To hate, to discriminate against those who look different, who talk different, who have different national backgrounds, or who act differently from the dominant group, is a universal trait of human nature. I say that there is only one possible solution and that is a vital experience with Christ on the part of all races. In Christ the middle wall of partition is broken down, the Bible says. There is no Jew or Gentile, or black or white or yellow or red. We could be one great brotherhood in Christ. However, until we come to recognize Him as the Prince of Peace, and receive His love in our hearts, the racial tensions will increase.

Prayer For The Day:

*I pray for Your love,
Lord Jesus, to conquer hate or prejudice—
whenever these ugly transgressions seep into my heart.*

·DECEMBER 18·

*"Except a man be born again,
he cannot see the kingdom of God."*

John 3:3

A person is saved by trusting in the finished work of Christ on the cross, and not by bodily sensations and religious ecstasy. But you will say, "What about feeling? Is there no place in saving faith for feeling?" Certainly, there is room for feeling in saving faith. But we are not saved by it. Whatever feeling there may be is the result of saving faith, but feeling never saved a single soul. Love is feeling. Joy is feeling. Inward peace is feeling. Love for others is a feeling. Concern for the lost is a feeling. But these feelings are not conversion. The one experience that you can look for and expect is the experience of believing in Christ.

Prayer For The Day:

*Thank You, Lord, for Your gift of
redemption, which does not fluctuate like my feelings.*

·DECEMBER 19·

*"What joy there is for anyone whose sins
are no longer counted against him by the Lord."*

Romans 4:8 (TLB)

A number of years ago I was stopped for driving too fast in a speed zone, and in the courtroom I pleaded guilty. The judge was not only friendly but embarrassed for me to be in his court. The fine was ten dollars. If he had let me go free, it would have been inconsistent with justice. The penalty had to be paid either by me or someone else! Judgment is consistent with love. A God of love must be a God of justice. It is because God loves that He is just. His justice balances His love and makes His acts of both love and justice meaningful. God could not consistently love men, if He did not provide for the judgment of evil-doers. His punishment of the evil-doer and His separation of the righteous is a manifestation of God's great love. We must always look at the cross on the dark background of judgment. It was because God's love for man was so intense that He gave His Son, so that man would not have to face judgment.

Prayer For The Day:

You are the Supreme Judge,
almighty God, and I thank You that
even though I did not deserve forgiveness, my judgment was paid
by Your beloved Son, Jesus Christ.

•DECEMBER 20•

"He was zealous for my sake . . ."
Numbers 25:11

I t is strange that the world accepts enthusiasm in every realm but the spiritual. The world appreciates and understands emotion and enthusiasm, until it becomes a religious fervor—then immediately it is suspect. When you bring a grand and glorious abandon to your dedication to the Lord Jesus Christ, you are thought by many of your neighbors to be mad, to have "gone too far" in religion. The whole history of missionary enterprise is filled with names like William Carey, Hudson Taylor, John Paton, David Livingstone, and others, who were thought by their generations to be mad. Their dedication was beyond the understanding of those who loved the smugness and the ease of contemporary life . . . And yet, in the last analysis, who are the mad ones? Are they not the complacent, self-centered, and smug who are so selfish that they tire of their own smugness, tire of their pleasures, and even tire of themselves?

Prayer For The Day:

Let me rededicate my life to You,
with complete abandonment, Lord Jesus.

• DECEMBER 21 •

*"Blessed is the man who reveres God, but the man
who doesn't care is headed for serious trouble."*

Proverbs 28:14 (TLB)

A ll Christians believe in God, but many Christians have little
time for God. They are too busy with everyday affairs to be
taken up with Bible reading, prayer, and being thoughtful to their
fellowmen. Many of them have lost the spirit of a zealous disciple-
ship. If you ask them if they are Christians, they would probably
answer, "I think so," or, "I hope so." They may go to church at
Easter and Christmas and on other special occasions, but otherwise
they have little time for God. They have crowded God out of their
lives. The Bible warns against neglect of your soul. It is possible to
harden your heart and shrivel your soul, until you lose your appetite for the things of God. This hunger, then, that you should have
is a desire to be always right with God. It is a consciousness that all
searching for peace of heart except in Him is in vain.

Prayer For The Day:

I hunger today to know more of You, Lord.

• DECEMBER 22 •

*"He that spared not His own Son, but delivered
him up for us all, how shall he not freely
give us all things?"*

Romans 8:32

G od is the Giver of the gift. The capability of the donor usually gauges the value of the gift. We don't usually think of a
person as a gift, but actually interpersonal relationships are the
most valued and cherished gifts of all. But the Bible teaches that
God gave a Person as a gift to every one of us, and that Person is
Jesus Christ. One day a six-year-old boy in a southern town answered a knock at the door. It was his father, just returned from
Southeast Asia. He didn't ask, "Daddy, what did you bring me?"
He threw his arms around his father's neck and said, "Oh, Daddy,
this is the best Christmas present I've ever had!"

Prayer For The Day:

*Your costly gift of Jesus, Father,
fills all the longings and desires of my heart.*

•DECEMBER 23•

*"For unto us a child is born . . . and his name shall
be called Wonderful, Counselor, The Mighty God,
The Everlasting Father, The Prince of Peace."*
                                                    Isaiah 9:6

To Christians the joy of Christmas is not limited to His birth. It
is built even more on the triumph of His death and resurrection—that gave meaning to His birth. The mysterious spirit of generosity which possesses us at Christmas is the afterglow of Calvary.
The fact of the cross illuminates this day and hallows it. As we
exchange our gifts, let us remember that they are symbolic of the
unspeakable gift of God's love. I do not believe that Christians
should be giving expensive gifts to each other. We should quietly
give simple little gifts that are expressions of our love and devotion
to the recipients. These gifts become symbolic of the gift of God's
love. How much money could be saved and invested in the Kingdom of God by thousands of Christian families every year if the
true meaning of Christmas was observed.

Prayer For The Day:

*Loving God, my heavenly Father,
in Your gift of Jesus I see Your immeasurable
love reaching out to all mankind. How I praise You and adore You!*

•DECEMBER 24•

*"When the fullness of the time was come,
God sent forth . . . his Son . . ."*
                                                    Galatians 4:4

Christmas is not a myth, not a tradition, not a dream. It is a
glorious reality. It is a time of joy. Bethlehem's manger crib
became the link that bound a lost world to a loving God. From that
manger came a Man who not only taught us a new way of life, but
brought us into a new relationship with our Creator. Christmas
means that God is interested in the affairs of people, that God loves
us so much that He was willing to give His Son.

Prayer For The Day:

*Lord Jesus, as I remember
Your birth in such a lowly stable,
cleanse my heart that it might be a sanctified gift for You.*

•DECEMBER 25•

*"And suddenly there was with
the angel a multitude of the heavenly
host, praising God . . ."*

Luke 2:13

When at this season of the year we wish our friends a "Merry Christmas," it is essential to realize that true merriment of heart is contingent upon the recognition of the truth that Christ was born in Bethlehem for our salvation. The word "merry" is from an old Anglo-Saxon word which sometimes meant "famous," "illustrious," "great," or "mighty." Originally, to be merry did not imply to be merely mirthful, but strong and gallant. It was in this sense that gallant soldiers were called "merry men." Favorable weather was called "merry weather." Brisk winds were called a "merry gale." Spenser speaks of London as "merry London." The word "merry" carries with it the double thought of "might" and "mirth," and is used both ways in Scripture. One of the early Christmas carols was "God Rest You Merry, Gentlemen." The Christian is to engage in spiritual merriment as he thinks upon the fact that, through the redemption, he becomes a child of God's family. The Bible teaches that the angels made merry at Christ's birth.

Prayer For The Day:

*This Christmas my heart is indeed
merry when I think of Your birth, dear Lord.
I rejoice with the angels and praise Your holy name!*

•DECEMBER 26•

*"Blessed is the man who trusteth in the Lord,
and whose hope the Lord is."*

Jeremiah 17:7

The Scriptures predict that a new day is coming. There will be a golden age of prosperity when all perplexing problems—religious, social, or political—will find their complete solution. It will be a marvelous time for this mixed-up world. However, the Bible teaches that man will not bring about this coming golden age. Man alone cannot. The flaw in human nature is too great. Man has no ability to repair this damaged planet. God is our only hope! His plans are already formed, and they are perfectly stated in the Scriptures.

*All my hope and plans
are laid at Your feet, Lord Jesus.*

•DECEMBER 27•

*"The Lord will bless
his people with peace."*

Psalm 29:11

How do we find peace with God? We must stop fighting! We must surrender! We must serve! Of course, these steps will be motivated by faith and mingled with love. Having found peace *with* God, next we experience the peace *of* God. This peace of God is not a mere abstraction advocated by preachers and theologians. Thousands of people can witness that they have actually experienced the peace of God and have found it wonderfully adequate for this present day. "For He is our peace."

Prayer For The Day:

*Father, I thank You for the peace You have
given to me, which does not depend on feelings or circumstances.*

•DECEMBER 28•

*". . . preaching peace by
Jesus Christ (he is Lord of all)."*

Acts 10:36

Would it not be wonderful if we could find an absolute cure for the troubles of human nature? Suppose we could give a shot in the arm to the whole human race that would fill people with love instead of hate, with contentment instead of greed. Suppose, also, a cure could be found for the past mistakes, failures, and sins of mankind. Suppose by some miracle all the past could be straightened out, all of life's tangles could be unraveled, and the broken strings of life could be repaired. The most thrilling news in all the world is the fact that there is a cure! A medicine has been provided! The sin, confusion, and disillusionment of life can be replaced by righteousness, joy, contentment, and happiness. A peace can be imparted to the soul that is not dependent on outward circumstances.

•DECEMBER 29•

*"A tenth of the produce
of the land . . . is the Lord's."*
Leviticus 27:30 (TLB)

We are to be stewards of our money. When it is invested and shared for the glory of God, it can be a boon and a blessing. I know a businessman in Detroit, Michigan, who made a promise to God that he would tithe his entire income to the work of the Lord. He said his business had tripled, and that God had more than fulfilled His end of the bargain. Some time ago I heard from a laborer in the San Joaquin Valley of California who said that he and his wife agreed to give one tenth of their income to the Lord. At the time they made their decision, he was able to get work only about seven months out of the year. Now he says he has steady work, and is earning nearly twice what he was before. You cannot get around it; the Scripture promises material and spiritual benefits to the man who gives to God. You cannot out-give God. I challenge you to try it and see.

Prayer For The Day:

*Forgive me, Lord, for the times
I have wanted to keep that which is rightfully Yours.*

•DECEMBER 30•

*"These are written, that
ye might believe that Jesus is the
Christ, the Son of God . . ."*
John 20:31

God caused the Bible to be written for the express purpose of revealing to us God's plan for his redemption. God caused the Book to be written that He might make His everlasting laws clear to His children, and that they might have His great wisdom to guide them, and His great love to comfort them as they make their way through life. For without the Bible this world would indeed be a dark and frightening place, without signpost or beacon. The Bible easily qualifies as the only book in which God's revelation is contained. There are many bibles of different religions; there is the Mohammedan Koran, the Buddhist Canon of Sacred Scripture, the Zoroastrian Zend-Avesta, and the Brahman Veda . . . They all begin with some flashes of true light, and end in utter darkness. Even the most casual observer soon discovers that the Bible is radically different. It is the only Book that offers redemption to us and points the way out of our dilemma.

Prayer For The Day:

> *Lord Jesus, as I read Your Word, Your*
> *truth shines through and illuminates a dark world.*

•DECEMBER 31•

> *"We know how much God loves us*
> *because we have felt his love . . ."*
> *1 John 4:16 (TLB)*

Never question God's great love, for it is as unchangeable a part of God as is His holiness. Were it not for the love of God, none of us would ever have a chance in the future life. But God is love! And His love for us is everlasting. The promises of God's love and forgiveness are as real, as sure, as positive, as human words can make them. But, like describing the ocean, its total beauty cannot be understood until it is actually seen. It is the same with God's love. Until you actually possess true peace with God, no one can describe its wonders to you.

Prayer For The Day:

> *Yes, almighty God, I have*
> *felt the consolation of Your love!*

Subject Index